Rural Social Work Practice

in Scotland

Colin Turbett

VENTURE PRESS

Published by
VENTURE PRESS
16 Kent Street
Birmingham
B5 6RD
www.basw.co.uk

British Library Cataloguing-in-Publication Data
A catalogue record for this book is available from the British Library

ISBN: 978-1-86178-083-6 (paperback)

Printed by:
Hobbs the Printers Ltd
Brunel Road
Totton
SO40 3WX

Printed in Great Britain

Contents

List of tables and figures

Tables

Figures

Acknowledgements

Thanks must go to the following who have provided assistance either directly or indirectly with this project. First, all the members of the 'Arran Team': not just my social services colleagues, but also all those in education, health, the police and the voluntary sector on the island. Collectively, I must thank my colleagues in the trade union, UNISON, and particularly those on the UNISON Scotland Social Work Issues Group. There are many others including, particularly, Shamus McPhee, Roseanna McPhee and Ken MacLennan (Scottish Gypsy Traveller Law Reform Coalition), Susan McVie (Edinburgh University), Jack Murchie (farmer, Arran) and Ruth Stark (BASW Scotland). Finally, thanks to my colleagues Maggie Rands and Diana Turbett (Arran), Catherine Johnston (Eilean Siar) and Kate Ramsden (Aberdeenshire) who looked at draft chapters and offered helpful comment from their own practice experience.

List of abbreviations

ASBO	Anti-Social Behaviour Order
BASW	British Association of Social Workers
BBC	British Broadcasting Corporation
CCTV	Closed circuit television
CHSCP	Community Health and Social Care Partnership
CRE	Commission for Racial Equality
ECHR	European Convention on Human Rights
EDM	Early Day Motion
EHRC	Equality and Human Rights Commission (successor to CRE)
EU	European Union
GIRFEC	Getting It Right For Every Child
GP	General Practitioner
GTEIP	Gypsy Traveller Education and Information Project
HEAT	Health improvement, Efficiency, Access and Treatment
IFSW	International Federation of Social Workers
ILF	Independent Living Fund
KPI	Key Performance Indicator
LGBT	Lesbian, Gay Bisexual and Transgendered
MARS	Multi Agency Resource Service
MP	Member of Parliament
MSP	Member of the Scottish Parliament
NAHWT	National Association of Health Workers with Travellers
NCH	National Children's Homes
NFWI	National Federation of Women's Institutes
NHS	National Health Service
OT	Occupational Therapist
PA	Personal Assistant
SBC	Shifting the balance of care
SGTLRC	Scottish Gypsy Traveller Law Reform Coalition
SOA	Single Outcome Agreement
SSKS	Social Services Knowledge Scotland
SSSC	Scottish Social Services Council
STEP	Scottish Traveller Education Programme
STUC	Scottish Trades Union Congress
SWIA	Social Work Inspection Agency
UK	United Kingdom
US	United States
WTE	Whole time equivalent

Introduction

Rural Social Work Practice in Scotland has been unconsciously in the making over a long number of years. Postgraduate study at Paisley University between 1999 and 2002 led to a realisation that there might be a gap in the literature. Whilst a number of texts address various aspects of social work practice in Scotland, none looks specifically at the rural context. Discussion amongst colleagues who were interested in the available international rural social work literature suggested that this project might be of interest. As such, it builds on previously published papers that were guided and influenced directly by the Welsh academic Richard Pugh, and by other writers such as Emilia Martinez-Brawley; I owe them a huge debt, but any errors in this book are entirely mine.

This book is not intended to be an encyclopedia about social work in rural Scotland. It will argue that social work practice draws generally from the same tools, methods, values and philosophies wherever practised. What does change when one works in a remote rural area is the context of practice, and this is true for other professional groups as well as social workers: living and working in the same place has implications for health workers, education staff and police officers, and all other human services workers. This book will concern itself with (to borrow from a well-known United Kingdom [UK] social work reader: Adams *et al.*, 2002) the *themes*, *issues* and *critical debates* surrounding social work practice in rural and remote Scotland.

The book will not cover practice with every service user group. This is less to do with space than with purpose. There will, for example, be little coverage of issues surrounding alcohol abuse – a huge problem in rural Scotland. The methods and resources required to help individuals (and their families and neighbours) address alcohol problems and their consequences, will be similar in any setting. However, the remote and rural context throws up its own issues: visibility, social exclusion, and access to services. These themes *will* be examined in the book. Similarly, the issue of how to safely convey detained mental health patients from their remote rural homes to acute psychiatric hospital many miles away, has in the recent past been a major issue addressed in a government-sponsored inquiry and report (Kerr, 2003). That issue, however, is primarily one for health agencies, and as this book is designed to look at the particular responsibilities of social workers in social care agencies, it is not discussed. However, issues connected with service delivery, stigmatisation and anonymity for service users with mental health problems will be examined.

Chapter 1 examines the broad context of social policy and the challenges for rural and remote practitioners. Chapter 2 examines practice and will introduce the reader to the international literature on rural social work. This has never been widely read in Scotland and at this stage in the early twenty-first century its influence on practice is at most marginal. Some rural practitioners, however, through their own study at undergraduate or postgraduate levels have discovered that out there is a rich vein of ideas and experiences with real meaning for a social work that does not fit the prescriptions of urbo-centric practice. Such writings come in the main from Australia, Canada and the United States (US) and these will be examined where relevant. The themes that pervade the international rural social work literature cover not just negative rural issues such as isolation, dual relationships, rural poverty and homelessness, but also the positives such as community identity, partnership working, environmental awareness and resourcefulness. Together, such aspects of rural practice can offer wonderful opportunities for practitioners that are rarely found in urban settings.

Chapter 3 looks at work with children and families, and Chapter 4 at work with adults. Chapter 5 looks at minorities and, in particular, the place of Scottish Gypsy Travellers in Scottish society. This particular focus is a departure from the depth of coverage other themes are given in the book, but is justified by the dearth of reference elsewhere in the available literature. Arguments in this chapter are delivered with some passion and it is hoped that the reader will forgive me if this seems at times to border on the polemical. Emphasis on particular themes in other sections of the book is considered justified for the same reason – lack of coverage elsewhere. Chapter 6 looks at management and organisational issues, including the use of new technology. Chapter 7 will draw conclusions and consider the future of rural social work as a genre in Scotland.

Chapter 1

Scotland: Social Work, Public Services and Rurality

Introduction

Social work in remote and rural areas does not operate in a vacuum: even the remotest island practitioner must now work within a framework prescribed by European, UK and Scottish government policy. This chapter will focus on the context of rural social work in Scotland with a brief overview of the main social policy drivers, official definitions of rurality, the changing economic context and the challenges for social care delivery within funding frameworks.

There are several issues around in Scotland as we enter the second decade of the twenty-first century that form a necessary background to the study of any aspect of public services:

- *The onslaught on public services* engendered by a shortage of government funds in the wake of the worldwide banking crisis in 2008: politicians of all the mainstream parties now accept that funding the bailout of the banks to the tune of billions of pounds of public money, had to come from somewhere. Opinions differ but the political editor of the influential *Local Government Chronicle* estimated in August 2009 that cuts in council spending in the UK might be in the region of 30 to 40 per cent (Drillsma-Millgrom, 2009), whilst Audit Scotland, the government advisory body on public fund accountability, considers that the overall Scottish Budget will be cut by between 7 and 13 per cent (Audit Scotland, 2009). 'Tough choices' are now being made about public expenditure policy, and these were much debated around the Westminster election of May 2010. This reduction in public spending is accompanied by population projections in Scotland indicating a growth in the numbers of dependent older people and a proportional decline in the numbers of people of working age available to look after them (see later in this chapter 'Challenges for social care'). The 'doing more-for-less' that had been a central theme of the 'new public management' (or managerial) discourse of the 1990s (see below and Chapter 6) has gained a new imperative.

- *'Welfare' to 'Workfare'*: over the past ten years or so, the UK, in common with other developed countries, has moved away from 'welfare' state provision where the state concerned itself with collective responsibility for the wellbeing of all citizens. Instead, we are experiencing the development of what has been described as the 'workfare' state (McDonald, 2006). This replaces a commitment to provide full employment with a 'workfare' policy that engages the unemployed (regardless of disability or other disadvantage) in job preparation and job seeking. This supposedly promotes flexibility in an open market-driven economy. The policy is exemplified by a system of state-provided, and private and purchased, benefits: at the bottom of the pile are asylum seekers who, being non-citizens, are denied the opportunity to work and therefore allotted only minimal sub-poverty line benefits (Dominelli, 2007); at the top are pensioners who have been fortunate enough to purchase private pension schemes based on well-paid employment when they worked prior to retirement. As this is written the government has announced plans to change the rules for claiming from the Independent Living Fund (ILF), a benefit for the most seriously disabled and dependent members of the community. In future, claimants will only be able to claim ILF if they work 16 hours or more per week; under current rules, according to news reports, only four claimants in Scotland out of the many hundreds who currently receive the benefit, would qualify. The implications in rural areas for 'workfare' policies generally are clear: acute disadvantage to sections of the population who are denied benefits but also unable to access distant employment and training opportunities. They are surrounded in some cases by relatively wealthy pensioners who have sought out the rural setting in retirement. Those who can access employment can find themselves forced into part-time, minimum-waged and insecure jobs.

• Linked with the context of the first bullet point, and flowing from developments worldwide in the past few decades, is *devolvement of decision making* to more local levels. Scotland now has its own Parliament with powers to determine the shape of social legislation, and potential opportunity to provide services that meet the particular needs of the population (Waterhouse and McGhee, 2002). This has seen differences emerge with policy elsewhere in the UK – free personal care for older people being the best-known example. Whether what was arguably a popular sop to the middle classes will outlive the financial crisis remains to be seen. Tax raising remains (with minor variation) a UK government concern. These tensions may encourage further moves towards independence, or they may stultify them. From a social work perspective, Pugh and Thompson (1999) warn that smaller societies are not always inclined to recognise and incorporate particular interest groups – the 'Balkanisation' of policy might result in greater inequity.

• *Global warming* and climate change are likely to increasingly impact upon rural areas; this is already being experienced in terms of the effects of the weather, especially flooding, on communities and infrastructure in Scotland. In Australia, problems stemming from prolonged drought are the subject of discussion in the rural social work literature (e.g. Cheers *et al*, 2007). Similarly, manmade disasters (whether through terrorist acts such as the Lockerbie Pan Am bombing of 1988, individual acts such as the Dunblane Massacre of 1996 or environmental disaster caused through pollution) require increasingly sophisticated responses.

Within social work generally there are particular developments:

- The agenda set by *Changing Lives* (Scottish Executive, 2006) – a report into the future of social work in Scotland, the context of which had been shaped by low public expectation, poor morale and a recruitment and retention crisis. The attacks on social workers from government and media in the wake of recent child deaths such as that of Peter Connelly in England have not been mirrored to such a negative extent in Scotland (Brody, 2009). *Changing Lives* may turn out to have little lasting impact but its emphasis on developing the profession of social work has been universally welcomed and supported by politicians of all parties. *Changing Lives* made reference to rural and remote practice, but as we shall see later, its actual influence in this respect seems marginal.

- There is increasing development of *managerialism* within social work organisations: this involves competition within a marketplace, the contracting out of services, treating service users as consumers, the use of performance indicators to measure the success of organisations, doing more-for-less, increased scrutiny, and gatekeeping and rationing (Harris, 2007). These developments will be examined in Chapter 6.

- A major contemporary policy driver is the move towards *personalisation* and individual budgets: although this is not as advanced as in England it remains an aspiration across the social care spectrum and will influence the future shape of social care in Scotland (Leadbeater and Lownsbrough, 2005; Scottish Government, 2009h). This will be examined in detail in Chapter 4.

- *Technological advance* has changed the face of public services just as it has the entire economy. For those of us in social work for more than twenty years, this is staggering in its scale. Records and assessments are no longer private affairs tucked away in files in offices, but through electronic means are (with notional user consent) instantly scrutinised and shared across services and agencies. Service users have been encouraged to exercise their citizen rights to shape entire services as well as their own personal care plans. Some of this will be universally welcomed; however, the apparently accompanying rise in bureaucratic demand on time is being rightly challenged by social workers who consider that it cannot be right that they spend up to 80 per cent of their time at a computer rather than with service users (White, 2008). The digital revolution has to impact on the isolation of services that are spread across marginally populated areas, just as it does the economy of such areas. This will be discussed in Chapter 6.

- *Specialisms* have become the norm over the past twenty years or so. Within them there is increasing fragmentation so it is not uncommon to find centralised services dealing with quite circumscribed aspects of service-user presentation. This applies within children and family and community care settings and seems to be a trend internationally (Cheers *et al.*, 2007). In Scotland this is associated with a complex system of European, UK and Scottish legislation governing activity; one author counted 48 separate pieces of primary legislation, with 53 major policy and other documents relating to children alone (Hothersall, 2008).

- Another pervading development is the universality of *eligibility criteria* that prescribe who gets a service and who does not (Harris, 2003). Early intervention and upstream development are seen as the preserve of universal services (often located within education or health services) that are also overstretched and under-resourced. This removes such responsibility from the trained and skilled social workers who were seen in the past as best placed to engage in such strategy (Smale *et al.*, 2000).

Defining rurality

Before a start is made on exploring issues against these background themes, it is important to define rurality in the Scottish context. Urban and rural areas are defined officially in Scotland as in Table 1.1.

Table 1.1 Scottish Government urban/rural classification

Area	Classification
1. Large urban areas	Settlements of over 125,000 people.
2. Other urban areas	Settlements of 10,000 to 125,000 people.
3. Accessible small towns	Settlements of between 3,000 and 10,000 people and within 30 minutes drive of a settlement of 10,000 or more.
4. Remote small towns	Settlements of between 3,000 and 10,000 people and with a drive time of over 30 minutes to a settlement of 10,000 or more.
5. Accessible rural areas	Settlements of less than 3,000 people and within 30 minutes drive of a settlement of 10,000 or more.
6. Remote rural areas	Settlements of less than 3,000 people and with a drive time of over 30 minutes to a settlement of 10,000 or more.

Source: Scottish Government (2009a)

Reproduced under the terms of the Click-Use licence

This book is concerned particularly with social work services to those who live in areas within the last two of these categories, and the definitions will be used throughout the text i.e. *accessible rural* and *remote rural*. In 2007-2008, eighteen of Scotland's 32 local authority areas included populations in both (see Table 1.2).

Table 1.2 Local authority population percentages

Local authority	Accessible rural % of population	Remote rural % of population
Aberdeenshire	36.7	16.0
Angus	26.7	0.7
Argyll & Bute	7.8	44.9
Dumfries & Galloway	19.6	29.3
East Ayrshire	18.4	8.7
East Lothian	15.1	12.7
Eilean Siar	0.0	78.2
Highland	11.8	39.7
Moray	30.2	13.9
North Ayrshire	5.5	4.9
Orkney Islands	0.0	67.3
Perth & Kinross	34.8	12.3
Scottish Borders	26.8	23.8
Shetland Islands	0.0	70.0
South Ayrshire	18.2	4.1
South Lanarkshire	11.0	1.3
Stirling	27.3	7.3
Scotland	11.2	7.0

Source: Scottish Government (2009a)

Reproduced under the terms of the Click-Use licence

In total in 2008, 19% of Scotland's population lived in these accessible and remote rural areas (336,056 in remote areas and 617,953 in accessible rural areas) – a sizeable minority of almost a million people whose lives and heritage are important components of Scotland's identity. This population is scattered across 94 per cent of the landmass, including the truly remote fringes of the Highlands and Islands (Scottish Government, 2009b). Population density is illustrated in Figure 1.1.

Figure 1. 1 Scotland's population density by local authority area

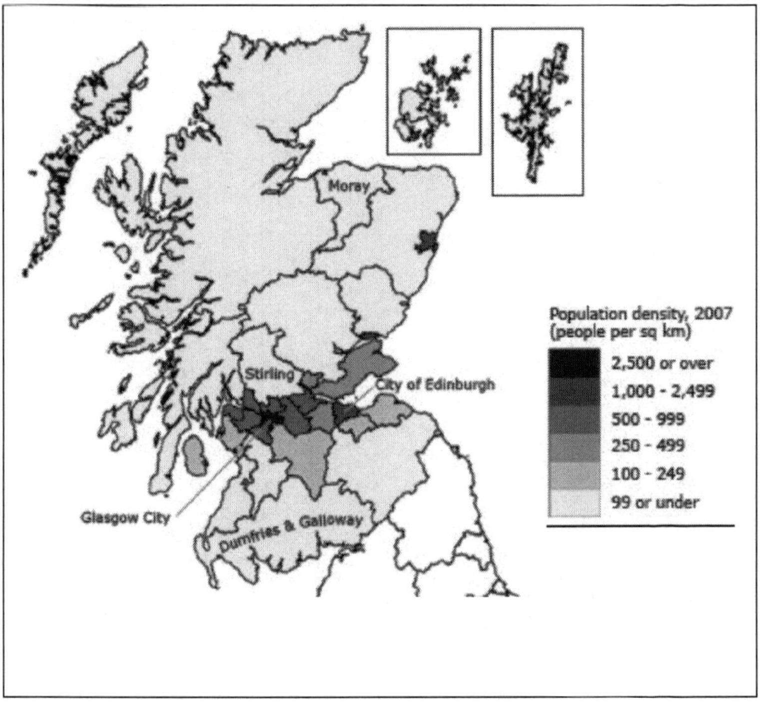

Source: Office for National Statistics (2008)

Reproduced under the terms of the Click-Use licence

Challenges for social care

The countryside and coastlines of Scotland are where, traditionally, we go for our holidays and for many of our leisure activities. It might be hard for outsiders to understand that behind the facade of beautiful scenery, big houses and holiday attractions there is an underbelly of social problems that can throw up as many issues for policy planners and service providers as anything found in our cities and their middle-class suburbs. Pugh (2003) discusses these issues in terms of 'contested space' where differences exist within rural communities about how life should be lived, about who should live there and about conservation and development (this theme will be developed in relation to young people in Chapter 3). Some of these themes are being tested around the question of land ownership, with communities in some remote areas using legal means to wrest control of the land and its resources from traditional landlords (Turbett, 2004). History is never far away: Scotland's Highlands and Islands were romanticised by the Victorians in the nineteenth century, masking a history of genocide and clearance that was still then under way. At the very time that Walter Scott was churning out his novels on Scottish history and Queen Victoria was building Balmoral Castle, Marx (1867) was writing of the terrible effect of the clearances on the ordinary people of the Highlands. When I travelled to Canada to study rural social care delivery in 2002, I met a succession of social workers and other human services professionals with Scottish surnames, whose ancestors, a few generations ago, had been forced through clearance or economic necessity to leave Scotland's Highlands and Islands (Hunter, 1994).

Scotland's rural communities face particular challenges in addition to the general pressures noted above: the importance of these have been outlined elsewhere in terms of their significance for the delivery of social work services (Turbett, 2009a):

• *A rural housing crisis.* Those dependent on welfare benefits, those on low pay and even those on public sector secure incomes are increasingly finding themselves squeezed out of the rural housing market. In one remote Scottish island, a recent report quoted a figure of over twice the average household income locally as being necessary for the purchase of a modest-sized family home (North Ayrshire Council, 2007). The collapse of the property-boom based economy in 2008 has not resulted in a significant decrease in housing prices. In September 2009 it was reported that rural Scottish housing prices were 17 per cent higher than urban ones, an increase in the differential of 3 per cent from figures released the previous year (The Herald, 2009). Seven per cent of homes in rural Scotland are second homes, supporting the notion that rural housing continues to be regarded as a speculative investment opportunity (Cloke *et al.,* 2002) – a trend evident in rural US as well as the UK (Rollinson and Pardeck, 2006). This trend is more pronounced in remoter rural areas where over 12 per cent of the housing stock are second homes. Recent research from the 2001 Census shows that the availability of socially rented housing in rural Scotland is in inverse proportion to the numbers of second and holiday homes (Communities Scotland, 2005). The overall rural housing problem, which affects workforce recruitment, has been described by the housing campaigning charity Shelter as so serious that 'rural life as we know it is under threat' (Shelter, 2004, p. 2). This has resulted in government attention to try and ensure that affordable housing is more readily available to those who live and work in rural areas (e.g. Scottish Government, 2009d).

• *Low pay and poverty in rural areas.* Whilst worklessness in Scotland tends to be associated with the urbanised and former industrial heartlands of West Central Scotland, low pay is most prevalent in the rural areas of Dumfries and Galloway, Moray and Clackmannan. Other poverty indicators also feature highly in remote rural areas: low income for those aged over 60, deaths of those aged under 65, chronic ill-health amongst those aged under 65, and 16- to 65-year-olds seeking paid employment (Palmer *et al.*, 2006).

• *A changing rural ooonomy.* Soventy fivc pcr cent of the landmass in Scotland is said to be under agricultural production, employing 65,000 people directly and a further 250,000 indirectly (NFU Scotland, 2010). Numbers who work on the land, the traditional source of income in rural areas, are in decline, especially amongst those who are engaged in farming full time – down from 44,044 in 1982 to 24,379 in 2009 (Scottish Government, 2010a). The largest employment source in accessible and remote rural areas is the public sector (20 and 19 per cent respectively), with 'education, health, social work and other community, social and personal services' accounting for two thirds of these jobs (Scottish Government, 2009c).

• *An ageing population.* Gross population imbalance looms in rural areas with obvious challenges to those planning services for older people. It is predicted that by 2024 the population aged over 65 will have risen in Scotland by 39.7 per cent from the 2007 figure, and those over 75 years old by 75 per cent. At the same time, the population of people of working age will fall by 5.2 per cent. In the sparsely populated Highland Council area with its proportionally large population of remote rural dwellers, the population aged over 65 will rise by an estimated 62.1 per cent, whilst the working age population of under 65s will fall by 7.2 per cent (figures from GROS, 2005, revised 2007). These figures are similar for most other remote rural areas and point towards a demographic time bomb with very problematic workforce issues in years to come (Smith and Homer, 2009).

• *Transport problems exaggerating geographical isolation.* Dependence on poor public transport systems can result in difficulty in accessing a range of opportunities almost taken for granted in urban areas, for example employment choices, healthcare and social services, food shopping, social and leisure activities and advisory services. Transport disadvantages *contribute* to social disadvantage in urban areas, but *cause* it in rural areas (Commission for Rural Communities, 2006). In health studies this has been described as 'distance decay': the further the user is from the source of the service, the lower the take-up, with obvious negative health consequences for the populations affected (Asthana *et al.*, 2003). In remote rural areas only just over half the population are within a fifteen-minute drive of a shopping facility, and 14 per cent live more than a fifteen-minute drive from a general practitioner (GP). The poor are more likely to own a car in rural areas and are more likely to spend a greater proportion of their income on transport (Pugh *et al.*, 2007). Post offices are the most accessible public service in Scotland – in 2006 all of us are said to have lived within a fifteen-minute drive of one (Scottish Government, 2009c); this is a service that is under threat in many areas – 30 rural post offices in Scotland were announced for closure in January 2008 (BBC News Highland, 2008). For those who do not have cars the situation is worse in rural areas: in remote areas 20 per cent in 2006 were within fifteen minutes of shops and 38 per cent within fifteen minutes of their GP (Scottish Government, 2009c).

Many of these issues are not specific to Scotland and are recognised as challenges throughout the European Community, even though the 'literature base around specific activities of social services in rural areas is surprisingly limited and compartmentalized' (Manthorpe and Livsey, 2009, p. 19). The authors of the scoping review just quoted, acknowledge that this lack of an evidence-base to inform practice on a pan-European basis will 'not serve practitioners or policy makers well' (ibid p. 19), presumably because so many funding opportunities and a lot of policy direction now comes from Europe.

Recognition of rurality and funding mechanisms

In England the government has an official policy of 'rural proofing' service developments This is applied to all policies, programmes and initiatives that stem from government departments and related agencies. Rural proofing compels policy makers to systematically:

* consider whether their policy is likely to have a different impact in rural areas, because of rural circumstances or needs;
* make a proper assessment of those impacts, if they are likely to be significant;
* adjust the policy, where appropriate, with solutions to meet rural needs and circumstances. (The Countryside Agency, 2002)

In Scotland the devolved government has a similar commitment but without a formal rural proofing policy. Instead, it has 'mainstreamed' the needs of rural Scotland within all its policies (Scottish Government, 2009g). This has been criticised for failing to properly involve rural people at grassroots level to ensure effective rural proofing through community capacity building – effectively ensuring that urban agendas dominate the agenda (Scottish Consumer Council, 2007).

The local delivery of services through local authorities is now determined by individually negotiated and signed Single Outcome Agreements between the Scottish Government and each of the 32 councils. This has involved the removal of ring-fenced funding for most services, allowing councils more flexibility in determining how to meet needs in their areas (but also a way of evading some agendas from central government that they might feel have little relevance for their localities, as we shall see in Chapter 5).

The major issue associated with rural funding mechanisms in Scotland is the method by which funds are allocated by the Westminster government to public services in the first place – the 'Barnett' formula. This allocates more per-head funding in Scotland than in England and includes recognition of the rural and population sparsity dimension arising from Scotland's geography (Twigger, 1998). However, funding in Scotland has been criticised on several levels: King et al. (2007) considered from their research that the formula used to compare English and Scottish relative need (upon which Barnett allocations are based) might be flawed, and should be reviewed. Midwinter (2006) calculated that funding allocations fall far short of needs – as high as 87 per cent for community and residential care services (primarily for older people) and 63 per cent for children's services. Additional demands are, in part, from the proliferation of legislation passed by the first two Scottish Parliaments (Association of Directors of Social Work, 2005). Within the rural context, Pugh et al. (2007) reviewed research reports concerning the provision of rural social care, and cautioned that UK funding mechanisms for resource allocation to public services have disadvantaged rural populations. They fail, for instance, to properly take into account factors such as geography, population scarcity and travel time for workers.

Key summary points

■ Scotland's social care services in rural areas in the first quarter of the twenty-first century will be influenced by an atmosphere of how *we can do more* (with an ageing population) *with less* (fewer resources in the public sector and fewer younger people proportionally in the population to provide formal and informal care).

■ Devolvement of government gives a greater opportunity to provide locally shaped services.

■ Communication technology, specialism and the emphasis on eligibility criteria all offer constraints but some possibilities for the development of services.

■ At 20 per cent of the population, remote rural dwellers are a significant minority living in 94 per cent of the country's landmass.

■ A number of factors of disadvantage indicate that there is an important place for services provided by social workers in remote rural areas: poverty, housing crisis, isolation and significant transport issues. However, there is at present little substantive literature evidence in Europe to support arguments for investment in such services and funding mechanisms remain contentious.

Chapter 2

Models and Issues in Rural Social Work Practice

Introduction

This chapter reviews the literature on rural social work practice as it particularly applies in the Scottish context. It examines the differences in emphasis that mark out remote and rural practice from that experienced in urban settings and points to some of the possibilities as well as problems that are a consequence.

Urban-rural difference

The question of whether there is or has ever been a difference between urban and rural social work practice has long been debated and the general consensus is that social workers work in much the same way wherever they are based (York *et al.*, 1998). The international literature on rural social work, which will be referred to particularly in this chapter, discusses the special characteristics of rural communities. Some of the descriptions of rural people and their lives, especially in some of the more post-modern inspired texts of Martinez-Brawley (2000) and Cheers (1998) (whilst being superb in other respects), emphasise a rather romanticised and idyllic image of rural people and their lives, and have been criticised as such (Lohmann and Lohmann, 2005b; Boyd and Parr, 2008). The danger of such texts is that they overplay differences in practice when the evidence suggests that such differences are largely contextual: as Lohmann and Lohmann (2005b, p. 315) (whose practice base in the US is working-class Appallachia rather than the conservative Mid-West) state, 'Good rural social work practice is, first and foremost, good social work practice'. Poor Scottish rural dwellers will undoubtedly have more in common with people in urban housing schemes than with their neighbours who enjoy affluence and privilege, even though this will be denied by certain rural lobby groups such as the Countryside Alliance (Turbett, 2004). The means used to tackle social problems will not therefore substantially differ, although the skills base of workers might, for reasons that will be described.

However, it has to be understood that the further one travels along the continuum that exists between densely populated urban areas and remote rural ones, the more the differences between both ends come into play; these differences concern such factors as the environment, access to services and inequities in service provision (Pugh, 2003; Lohmann and Lohmann, 2005b). These are examined in Chapters 3 and 4 relating to the principal service user groups. The international rural literature points to particular skills requirements and other considerations in the rural setting that are applicable to the Scottish context, and these will be explored in this chapter. The question of how rural models of practice can fit a Scottish perspective on social work in the twenty-first century, given all the macro and micro tensions described in Chapter 1, is the central theme of this book.

Generic practice and generalism

Before proceeding further with the discussion it is probably worth defining the difference between *generic* and *generalist* practice because of the danger of confusion. *Generic* practice has almost died out in Scotland (and the UK – as well as other countries with similar social work systems such as Australia, Canada and the US). In the UK it describes the worker who straddled the previous specialisms within the social work departments created as a result of the Kilbrandon Report and the Social Work (Scotland)

Act 1968 (Martinez-Brawley, 1984; Stevenson 2005). Bob Winter, the first director of Greenock Burgh Social Work Department, recalls in 1969 deliberately mixing the caseloads of the workers who came into his new department from their former specialist roles in the old Children's, Welfare and Probation Services (Bruce et al., 2009). However, by the mid-1980s, generic teams in Scotland had mostly been replaced by specialist ones and that fragmentation into increasingly specialised working practices has continued. This is said to have been preferred by social workers who found it difficult to keep abreast of increasingly complex practice across the groups of users who were demanding services (Martinez-Brawley, 1984). Generalism concerns a method rather than a field of practice and will be described in some detail below because of its continued prominence in the international literature on rural social work (Cheers, 1998; Ginsberg 1998b; Laine Scales and Streeter, 2004; Lohmann and Lohmann, 2005a; Collier 2006).

In 1986, rural and remote social work Scottish practice was reported by the international commentator Emilia Martinez-Brawley. Her study focused on the Isle of Barra at the southern end of the Western Isles (Eilean Siar) where a singleton practitioner undertook a variety of field social work tasks including some, such as the organising of the home help service, that would not be on the skills inventory of many social workers. Martinez-Brawley was particularly interested in the way in which her subject undertook community development and capacity building, a role that went beyond traditional casework. She also observed how living and working in a small community transcended boundaries and barriers normally found in social work practice. Intrusions on private life were taken for granted and accepted. A positive picture emerged with the main downsides being an absence of support and collegial relationships – carrying the danger of burnout (Martinez-Brawley, 1986). These are all themes that remain of relevance today.

The Barra study celebrated the idea of generalism as being the best fit for style and practice in rural settings. This notion has a long history in the literature of rural social work: in 1933, the US social worker Josephine Brown described a fusion of individual casework, networking with existing voluntary organisations and developing what we would now call citizen leadership that has continued in such writings internationally down to the present day (Brown, 1933). The idea that generalism should enjoy some primacy amongst rural practitioners because it allowed workers whose service users were often cut off from specialist services, to pick from an inventory of strategies, was founded on the reality of isolation and remoteness. The Canadian writer Collier describes generalism as follows:

The generalist considers problem solving on many levels, across a spectrum of conceptual and practical approaches, and pursues any avenue that may be productive. It is not a specific approach, like casework with its theoretical bases. The generalist enters each situation ready to tackle an individual problem, a neighbourhood issue or a political contest.

(Collier, 2006, p. 36-7)

Some writers have preferred the term 'multi-skilling' as what workers who engage in such practice are really doing is providing multiple services in multiple roles (Mason, 2006). However, there seems little doubt that Martinez-Brawley's description of working in the Outer Hebrides in 1985 has changed since that time: the autonomy and freedom to practise, to fit with community requirements, enjoyed by the social worker subject of her study, would hardly be recognised by today's practitioners anywhere in Scotland.

In the mid-1980s, social workers in Scotland operated under the structures of one major piece of legislation – the Social Work (Scotland) Act 1968 – which lent an enabling framework for practice rather than strict governance and procedure. Since then a number of major pieces of legislation have been passed that have complicated procedures and increased the weight and volume of assessments. Social workers in their various settings now need to know how to operate under the Children (Scotland) Act 1995, the Criminal Procedure (Scotland) Act 1995, the NHS and Community Care Act 1990, the Adults with Incapacity (Scotland) Act 2000, the Regulation of Care (Scotland) Act 2001, the Mental Health (Care and Treatment) (Scotland) Act 2003 and the Adoption of Children (Scotland) Act 2007. This list is intended to be illustrative rather than exhaustive, and there are various other pieces of legislation that are important to particular specialisms. In addition, eligibility criteria, as mentioned in Chapter 1, are now universal – in Children and Family settings these are laid down in the tiered intervention approach under *Getting It Right For Every Child* (GIRFEC) guidance (see Chapter 3) which states that social workers become involved in complex cases up to and including those where children are vulnerable or at significant risk of harm. With Adults a recent consultation exercise conducted by the Scottish Government is expected to lay down similar Scottish-wide guidance (Scottish Government, 2009e). If professional autonomy ever existed in social work it seems to have disappeared under the weight of all this prescriptive legislation.

Is all this really intended to mean that social workers cannot become involved in early intervention and community development strategies? Smale *et al.* (2000) caution that without the ability to undertake upstream work, social workers are like lifesavers trying to save a succession of drowning people in a river when what is required is to go 'upstream' to stop them jumping in to start with. They expand the metaphor by warning that specialist workers could become like these same lifesavers who, with different-coloured hats, can only save the drowning people who wear the same-coloured hat, so that the nearly drowned have to change hats to get attention if their particular lifesaver is busy! This was certainly not the intention of *Changing Lives* (Scottish Government, 2006). Its discussion on the role of social workers suggests that social workers have the skills to become involved in a variety of interventions up to and including those in Tier 4 at the top of the triangle diagram in Figure 2.1, which contains reserved functions.

Figure 2.1 Tiered intervention model

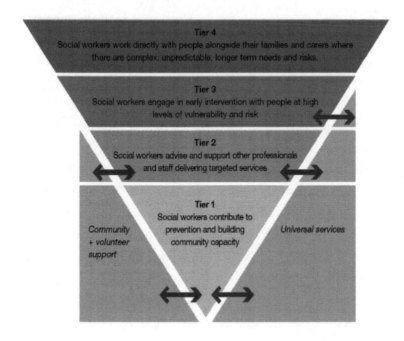

Source: Scottish Government (2006)

Reproduced under the terms of the Click-Use licence.

Have generic practice and generalism had their day? Is there still a place for a particular rural practice model or has communication technology made this redundant and reduced us all to similar urban-based practice styles? It is certainly the case that generic practice (in the sense of workers who practise across the various specialisms of adult and children service user categories) is now very rare and does not fit with contemporary graduate social work training. However, *Changing Lives* suggested that generic roles 'might be the best, or indeed, the only solution' to issues of providing services in remote locations (Scottish Government, 2006, p. 27). Whilst this was possibly shutting the stable door after the horse had bolted, it did at least gives implicit permission to explore what the best fit might be. In Eilean

Siar (the same Outer Hebrides that contains the locality studied by Martinez-Brawley) this seems to have gone in another direction. In response to an inquiry into a particular childcare case (discussed in Chapter 3) and a critical Social Work Inspection Agency (SWIA) Performance Inspection Report (SWIA, 2006), a restructuring has taken place that places social work with adults into one council department and social work with children and families into another (SWIA, 2008). Thus, in one of the smallest local authority social work agencies in Scotland, social workers are managed separately in different teams in different departments, perhaps denying structural opportunity for mutual support and sharing of work. Stevenson (2005, p. 570) argues that the true meaning of generic practice is that it 'rests upon the assumption that social work has a common base, in which values, knowledge and skills can be applied to a range of situations'. Structures in rural areas should be able to provide opportunities for such practice and not inhibit them.

Generalism also implies the use of imagination and innovation. These are qualities that are rarely discussed in social work literature, England (1986) being a notable exception. However, as we have seen, rural generalists will constantly invent solutions rather than take them off the shelf or refer on to a specialist. In this respect they enjoy areas of discretion akin to the descriptions by Lipsky (1980) of 'Street-level bureaucrats' that were thought by many to have disappeared along with professional autonomy as part of the managerialist thrust of the 1990s (Evans and Harris, 2004). Lipsky considered that discretion necessarily occurred in organisations where frontline workers were constrained by resource limitations, where demand was potentially limitless, and where accountability to the organisation depended very much on what was reported by the frontline worker. Whilst computer-led recording (and therefore monitoring) systems have sharpened accountability to the organisation, solution finding in the rural context still depends on the worker's ability to interpret policy and seek answers that will benefit the service user, because resources and onward referral options will be so limited.

Community-orientated practice

As we saw in the last section the generalist role is felt to fit rural and remote communities because social workers will encounter problems and issues that cannot simply be referred on to other agencies – the chances being that resources do not exist or if they do they are parachuted in from an urban centre somewhere else so infrequently, that their use is limited. The local social workers' knowledge of their community will be enhanced in many cases by the fact that this is also where they live and go about the non-working aspects of their lives. Martinez-Brawley and others have described this intervention possibility as 'community social work' or 'community orientation' (Martinez-Brawley, 1990, 1998, 2000; Cheers, 1998; Poole, 2005; Pugh and Cheers, 2010), involving a community development role as well as personal social work services. This certainly involves stepping outside the boundaries of prescriptive assessment and care management approaches to individual problems that are now standard across the specialisms in social work (Harris, 2003).

In Chapter 5 of this book, emphasis is put on the requirement for a human rights approach when working with minority ethnic groups. Ife (2008, pp. 116-19) contends that social workers should *always* consider appropriate community development approaches alongside traditional individual service ones, as this parallels the link between human rights and citizen obligation. Ife illustrates this idea by arguing that the right to vote and the right to joint trade unions were won through collective struggle and sacrifice; the trend for opting out of such rights through apathy, feeds a society in which history is forgotten and people live only for the present, to the detriment of democracy. This fine ideal can be translated into practice in a rural setting because opportunities will present themselves and social workers will find themselves able to influence engagement.

In the UK, 'community orientation' as a term belongs to the pre-Griffiths age of social work characterised by the movement for patch teams and localised working of the 1970s and 1980s (Smale and Bennett, 1989). It is interesting to note when looking back to such trends that this movement did address the debate about generic versus specialist practice within community teams, one survey concluding that specialisation amongst staff was a positive attribute so long as methods could be found within teams to share knowledge and skills (Hadley *et al.*, 1987). The rebirth of community-orientated practice as *community capacity building* seems to have brought us back full circle. The Scottish Government's overall vision for public service staff is clear:

> *Specialist staff who form a relationship with communities and groups, and support them over a period of time and through different stages of their development, play an important role in community capacity building. Other staff, working in a range of settings and providing an input to community capacity building as one part of their role, also contribute significantly (and also need specific skills in order to be able to do so effectively). The most effective capacity building is usually embedded into the process of helping communities take action towards their goals.*
>
> (Scottish Government, 2009f)

This is also recognised explicitly for social workers in *Changing Lives* (Scottish Government, 2006, p. 38), with the suggestion that community social work should be conducted with other agencies, such as education, housing, health and the police, as part of joint approaches 'at the heart of communities'.

Pierson (2008) differentiates between community-level and community-based services but is clear that they can be complimentary approaches: the former are aimed at helping whole communities through capacity building, whilst the latter are directed towards individuals and families through interventions that are community rather than centrally based. The rural generalist social worker will be necessarily involved in the latter but is also well placed to become involved in community capacity building, as both strategies will go hand in hand. There is an obvious tension here between different sets of expectations, with community capacity building perhaps in reality being seen as less of a priority than the real business of social workers, that is assessment and care management. However, rural and remotely based social workers may be better placed to take advantage of the opportunities this official sanction that *Changing Lives* gives, especially when it might not be the business of anyone else in a sparsely resourced remote area.

The actual business of effective community orientation might involve a team mapping exercise in which target areas are identified and then a plan developed to address them (Smale *et al.*, 2000). The team in this sense may be a single or multi-agency one, and can involve service users and carers. This was the method used by the the Badenoch and Strathspey social work team in the 1980s (Green, 1989, 1993). They identified a number of issues they felt underlay their workload, including a chronic shortage of housing and a general absence of a common understanding of problems amongst agencies that should have been working in partnership.

Community capacity building can involve building citizen leadership (a *Changing Lives* aspiration) in which community members are equipped to gain influence within decision-making processes, whether as user/carer representatives, or as residents in an area with commonly experienced social problems (e.g. transport issues, youth provision deficits). This can involve empowering individuals to rekindle skills that have lain dormant, or ensuring that a local committee or group are resourced and supported to function effectively at the most basic level: somewhere to meet, and administrative support. It might also involve raising the level of volunteering - peer mentors for young people at risk of school exclusion, starting up a youth centre or local youth forum, or setting up informal neighbourhood care or shopping schemes to benefit older people (Pierson, 2008).

Community capacity building, and indeed, empowering and imaginative social work, have been incorporated within the *Personalisation* agenda, a main thrust of UK and Scottish Government social policy (Leadbeater and

Lownsbrough, 2005). This seeks to help individuals and communities find their own solutions to social care issues rather than be forced through lack of choice to accept restrictive public provision. Whether this is either realistic or achievable will be discussed in Chapter 4.

The ability to put community-orientation into practice must be one of the most attractive elements of the rural and remotely based work setting. Some examples of community orientated practice are also given in Chapters 3 and 4.

Dual relationships

It is rare for social workers in urban areas to live in the areas where they work and most will make a conscious choice not to do so. This gives space from the working environment and makes it unlikely that there will be any overlap between family/personal life and working life. Many social workers would view such overlaps as at least potentially intrusive and stressful, especially if their work involves the type of confrontation typically found (but not exclusively) in children and family, and criminal justice work settings. There are no such possibilities for many workers in rural and remote settings and the issues that arise are complex and will be discussed in the remainder of this chapter.

The first of these concerns *dual relationships*. This concept explains the fact that people who share the same community space but who have a worker-service user relationship, are also likely to encounter one another in settings involving other types of relationship. This might be as simple as having your bins emptied by a service user, or being served by them in a shop. It might be more complex, involving the closer relationships that arise from being neighbours and perhaps friends with someone, or encountering them in another role through work. For some workers in remote communities it can involve the agency dealing with their own family members as service users. Reamer's classification of dual relationships is the one usually quoted in the contemporary literature (Galbreath, 2005;

Pugh, 2007) which attempts to clarify their nature in the rural context:

- intimate relationships (emotional and sexual);
- the pursuit of personal benefits (material, financial, etc.);
- professionals seeking to meet their own emotional needs through service users,
- altruistic gestures (attempts to help service users that go beyond one's usual professional role);
- unanticipated circumstances (chance encounters with service users in other settings).

This immediately highlights the more problematic dual relationships. The first two are clearly prescribed in the Codes of Practice that govern professional registration (Scottish Social Services Council, 2009) but all apart from the final one could, in their perceived transgression, potentially bring social workers into conflict with their employer and the Scottish Social Services Council as registration body. All will involve the rural worker in consciously defining boundaries with service users in a manner rarely required of urban-based workers. The transgression of such boundaries with vulnerable service users is fraught with hazards, including damaging consequences when a therapeutic relationship becomes a more personal and emotional one. The power inherent in the worker/service user relationship must be understood so that when boundaries are crossed in a potentially damaging manner this can be seen as abusive. One of the most obvious practical consequences is that the worker involved lets down their colleagues: the extra attention or service they are offering might be similarly expected of other workers and by other service users. This might especially be the case in a small community where, as we have observed elsewhere, little happens without comment from neighbours. Drawing from Miller (1998), Galbreath (2005) and Pugh (2007), let us examine the different types of dual relationships in turn.

Whilst *intimate relationships* with service users are clearly proscribed and this should be fairly easily understood even if not always avoided, the matter becomes less clear when intimate relationships with others could affect the relationship with the service user. This could arise from a number of circumstances: an intimate relationship with a colleague who is also involved with a service user (it is not unusual in rural settings for spouses to work in the same agency) might lead to suspicions of 'pillow talk'. Likewise, a worker might be personally involved with a member of the service user's wider family, or with some other person of significance to the working relationship. These are all likely to arise in the rural setting, especially if workers originate or have family ties there. Judgement, perhaps from discussion with supervisors or colleagues, will be required to ensure that there is no conflict of interest. This might also be difficult for a worker moving to a remote area whose partner becomes involved in other aspects of community, social or business life; it is also potentially restricting and problematic for single workers choosing with whom to have an intimate relationship in a small community.

The *pursuit of personal benefit* at first sight also appears to be clear. No one could argue that it would be legitimate to gain personally from any transaction involving a service user. The US literature discusses 'bartering' (Miller, 1998; Galbreath, 2005) whereby proud service users find it easier to accept services that are provided for free if they feel they are giving something back in kind: in a Scottish rural context it is not unusual to be sat down by an older person for formal tea, a cake and conversation, before getting down to business. This might be considered harmless, and little more than good manners, but is the handing over and graceful acceptance of garden or crofting produce any less problematic? The answer may lie in agreement about boundaries between worker and supervisor. Most public sector employers proscribe the acceptance of gifts of any more than token value, and this too will be a consideration.

The question of *professionals who seek to meet their own needs through clients* may be the one consideration that might apply regardless or rural or urban setting. There is little doubt that most human services professionals will find that their work can bring a sense of satisfaction and therefore personal reward. Again the guidance of supervisors is necessary if the worker finds their relationship with a service user goes beyond this into more personal areas e.g., if the service user is being looked to in order to more directly meet a need that the worker has, perhaps for therapeutic reasons.

Altruistic gesture is considered a very real danger in a remote or rural setting. A vulnerable service user might well misinterpret the kindness and interest of a social worker as an offer to develop a relationship that goes beyond that expected by the agency – a non-professional one. If the service user lives in the same community, they may not understand why the worker, whom they might encounter at any time, is not available to them whenever they wish to see them. This can lead to the raising of demands for attention, especially if the service user is alone and in crisis. If the worker responds by offering unconditional availability, the relationship becomes problematic and non-professional. This becomes even more blurred if the worker is also involved, as many remotely based workers are, in out-of-hours emergency cover. Management support and clear boundary setting are required to protect the worker and service user under such circumstances. In an article for the social work journal *The New Social Worker*, Handon (2009) suggests a list of inappropriate behavioural cues for concern on the part of supervisors. Most of these concern signs of intimate physical attraction, discussed briefly above. However, the list includes disclosure to a service user of personal contact details such as a mobile or home telephone number, email address or social networking site account. It also suggests that using personal funds to support a service user's needs (especially if the agency has refused) is inappropriate from a dual relationship aspect. Handon suggests that the families of service users might themselves alert agencies to such issues and it might be added that colleagues and workers from other agencies might also pass comment. These are all signs, at the very least, of altruistic gesture. Their resolution might be a supervision or training issue but if such measures fail to resolve matters, could become a registration and disciplinary one.

The likelihood of a social worker encountering a service user in *unanticipated circumstances* is very high in rural and remote settings. Shops, school parent nights and community facilities are examples of places where such encounters are likely to take place. This is unavoidable and should be harmless – but can result in embarrassment on both sides. Does the worker, for instance, acknowledge the other party, or do they follow the cue given by the service user, which might involve pretence that they do not know each other? The answer perhaps lies in prior agreement between the two about how to deal with such circumstances; indeed, many rural social workers make a point of this when agreeing a work plan with a new service user. On the other hand, the worker may find that the service user wishes to take advantage of the chance encounter by raising issues that arise from professional contact. This is not uncommon and will have to be addressed individually and sensitively: the difference between being on duty and going about one's other business in life may not be understood in a small community where roles are blurred and many people have several jobs (Turbett, 2004).

Confidentiality

The Scottish Code of Practice for registered social workers includes 'respecting confidential information and clearly explaining agency policies about confidentiality to services users and carers' (Scottish Social Services Council, 2009). This is a fairly clear statement that will be understood and generally accepted by social workers regardless of their setting. However, in a rural context the issues can be less clear. Martinez-Brawley (2000) explains that the absence of anonymity in a small community requires further consideration about the concept of confidentiality. The ethical standard, she argues, should be based upon what is best for a service user and what it is that they, the worker, the agency and even the whole community are trying to achieve. The classic psychotherapeutic worker-client relationship based standard, places limits on the rural social worker that might not be true to the goals they and the service user are trying to achieve.

The same section of the Codes that discusses confidentiality also demands that workers should be 'honest and trustworthy'. If one uses this correctly it might mean that confidentiality should be interpreted constructively rather than literally. Whilst it is easy to hide behind confidentiality and never offer comment on a situation we are privy to, are we always sure that this is in a service user's interest? Gossip in small communities has been described as a powerful force with both positive and negative characteristics (Cheers, 1998; Martinez-Brawley, 2000; Pugh 2000). It keeps information and news in circulation and certainly shapes community approval or disapproval of the actions of others; it thus performs a social regulatory role. In the positive sense it also allows people to vent frustration and test out opinion on others without having to own the statement being made as it always comes from some other source of unknown origin. In rural Scotland the phrase is often heard that 'what people do not know they make up' and it is here that gossip can be damaging.

Personally I have now worked so long in the same remote community where everyone knows my social work role, that few people make comment in my hearing about situations they think I might know about through work (they are often wrong!). However, when a statement is made that is clearly incorrect, and in being so, damaging to the service user under discussion, it might be considered appropriate to correct the information in circulation (Martinez-Brawley, 2000). It might be best to check this out with the subject first because, who knows, they may have started the story themselves for their own reasons. There may then be agreement about how the gossip could be corrected, or at the very least, enough doubt placed on its truthfulness, that this itself will be incorporated into its onward transmission.

A member of staff in my office recently told me that his son and a teenage friend had been discussing another youngster known to them within his obvious hearing: the friend commented that the other young person had been 'taken away and put in a home in Aberdeen'. In fact the young person had simply moved from a relative's home in the local community to his mother's new home elsewhere. The worker concerned made no comment about this rather alarming take on events, even though his son expected that he might. When he later told me about the incident I asked whether it might have been in the young person's interests (who was indeed known to social services) to at least shed some doubt on the story being circulated – perhaps along the lines of 'don't believe everything you hear'. Would this (not unusual) scenario for a rural worker have constituted a breach of confidentiality?

Another particular issue related to confidentiality for the rural social worker is how to deal with information picked up informally outside the work setting. This could happen in any social situation or simply through observation, or might arise from the transmission of gossip as discussed above. In some circumstances there will be a clear duty to refer it to the agency with a view to action being considered: this will be the case in relation to protection issues for children or vulnerable adults. In other circumstances discretion will have to be exercised – whilst we should not act on gossip we might want to take information back to a service user to check things out with them, depending on its significance for the area of work concerned. A study in Australia found this to be a significant issue for rural social workers, partly because there was no guidance available on the matter (Green and Mason, 2002).

There are thus two main issues in relation to confidentiality: that of the dilemmas for the rural worker who lives and works in the same locality (as discussed elsewhere in this chapter) and also that of issues arising from the particular way in which information is circulated in a rural community. This can result in workers coming under intense pressure over controversial decisions that are considered of public interest (Schmidt, 2005): that is indeed what happened in Orkney in 1991 in the situation described in Chapter 3.

Isolation

Although there may be few rurally based social workers in Scotland who are working entirely on their own, many will be based in small teams with perhaps only one or two colleagues undertaking the same type of work they do. There are a number of issues for such workers: geographical distance from peer support, from supervisory support and from training opportunity, can all be stressful and problematic. These factors will be exaggerated if there are also pressures locally that are pulling the worker away from the direction required by their agency. There are potentials for this in every area of field social work, as discussed in other chapters in this book.

Isolation in a remote area may also mean that there are few choices over resources that might benefit service users, whether to support them in their own homes or elsewhere if that becomes impossible. There may be few respite or daycare opportunities for old and disabled people requiring support, no local foster carers for children who require a period away from home but who could otherwise be safely and more appropriately accommodated within their home communities. The seeking out of alternative ways to meet need, or even the creation of required resources, may not fall within the remit of an urban-based worker, but for the rural generalist this will be a basic requirement of the job. Imagination and innovatory flair, as discussed earlier in this chapter, will be the order of the day.

Isolation may well be deliberately sought by the worker who opts for a remote work location and it would be unusual to find anyone who has not made that choice for their own reasons. In Scotland a remote location often goes hand in hand with a stunning environment and opportunities for outdoor activities in leisure time that might involve considerable travel in other settings. With that, however, comes personal sacrifice – especially if you like shopping or a choice of places to dine out. In the summer months there may be lots of new faces around as visitors fill the place up, but for the rest of the year it can seem a very small world indeed – and no place to hide. The same issue will apply to colleagues in health, the police and other human services, and often mutual support amongst the wider multi-disciplinary team can offset the availability of immediate peer support (Turbett, 2004). This is similarly reported by other disciplines (Schmidt, 2000; Wright, 2000). However, 'first names' between staff from different agencies can breed complacency – a belief that because we all know one another, we must be working together well even though there may not be much evidence of emerging good practice. Reflective inter-agency discussion can help avoid this possible problem. Informal networks might be enhanced by lunch clubs, in addition to well-focused team working over particular issues with families, individuals and groups. In the author's setting the authority's Child Protection Committee hosts well-attended meetings of workers from the police, health, education, pre-school providers as well as social services, on a regular basis, looking at the latest practice issues (including the lessons from inquiries) and discussing them in an informal atmosphere.

Workers who are expected to practise in geographical isolation from their peers in the profession require a high level of agency understanding, support and confidence (Turbett, 2009a). They also require good and effective supervision, and support with workload management. These features will be dealt with in more detail in Chapter 6.

The hows and whys of survival as a rural social worker

Lohmann and Lohmann (2005b) advise that if you can work effectively as a social worker in a rural area in the US you can work anywhere because you will have learned to be 'resourceful and creative', and it might be useful to consider practice in Scotland from this standpoint. What I think they mean by this is that there are not just particular skills required of the remote and rurally based worker, but also certain personal characteristics, and it is this combination that makes for a worker who can both cope with and enjoy the setting. Some of these have been touched on already in this chapter. In the US (as indeed in Australia and Canada), consideration has been given to this by educators. A number of authors provide inventories of skills and personal requirements of rural social workers (Cheers, 1998; Southern Regional Educational Board, 1998; Pugh, 2000; Krieg Mayer, 2001; Locke and Winship, 2005; Cheers *et al.,* 2007). Without claiming originality, I have drawn from the literature a list of requirements (or characteristics) that fit the Scottish context.

Rural social workers in Scotland need to:

1. be skilled at working in partnership with related professionals, as well as peers and other colleagues;
2. be able to undertake effective inquiry to understand the needs of a rural community;
3. understand the culture and customs of the community they are working in and utilise such knowledge in order to provide culturally sensitive services (this should not, however, reduce to a compromise on basic anti-discriminatory approaches, as will be seen in later chapters in this book);
4. have an ability to identify and mobilise resources at all levels to resolve local issues – community capacity building skills;
5. have an ability to meet their own professional personal development requirements through self-identification of gaps in knowledge, and ensure access to adequate resources or training;
6. have an ability to identify gaps and analyse strengths and weaknesses in the social care policies of their agencies and the governmental bodies that determine them;
7. have skills in bridging the gap between policy makers and the rural community at the receiving end, so that users and carers are able to influence policy;
8. be able to work in a variety of roles (i.e. generalist practice) as required by service users and carers, individually and in groups;
9. be able to provide technical assistance to community groups to help

them have a voice;

10. have the ability to conduct themselves personally in a rural community in a manner that wins trust and confidence, and communicates effectively with people;

11. have the ability to evaluate their own professional performance;

12. have skills in change management;

13. be able to contribute to knowledge about effective practice in rural areas;

14. be conscious of personal safety issues and be able to apply them for self and colleagues.

This is an ambitious list that represents an ideal aspiration rather than a checklist for potential applicants for rural posts, and covers areas discussed elsewhere in this chapter. It does, however, highlight the independence, self-motivation and breadth of skills required of the rural social worker who might be working in a situation of isolation, where there is no agency framework that necessarily meets these responsibilities for the worker.

The call for workers to conduct themselves in a certain way (no. 10) might seem almost an infringement on freedom; in an urban setting one's personal life is one's own as long as it does not contravene professional codes of conduct. In the US some texts suggest that the rural-based worker should be conforming to the general practices of the community, for example attending church and respecting other social norms (Ginsberg, 1998b; Watkins, 2004) if they wish to enjoy any influence. This social conservatism is also said to apply to dress and social behaviour, including such matters as alcohol consumption. However, the conservative rural heartlands of the US are not Scotland, and there are differences. Other writers (Cheers, 1998; Pugh, 2000) put more emphasis on the suggestion that influence and respect within a rural community are won quietly through hard work over a period and this seems to better fit the Scottish situation. In rural Scotland, nothing annoys longstanding residents more than the new arrival who immediately begins to noisily take over local community groups, as if their experience (often an urban one) was just what everyone had been waiting for. In the author's experience, lying low on arrival in a rural community seems to be more effective than sweeping in like the proverbial new broom, and once basic professional respect has been won, then other personal attributes are likely to be taken on board. Cheers (1998) advises that from the start, new workers should give people positive things to discuss about them, rather than negative things to critique, as such talk will happen anyway.

Rural communities in Scotland nowadays have diverse populations whose origins are often from elsewhere and acceptance of the worker as an individual is probably more likely than it might have been many years ago. This might be an uphill task if the worker's personal characteristics are not ones traditionally understood within small communities – being openly gay might be difficult in some communities, but not impossible. The main emphasis of self-presentation should be about being seen to be hard working, committed and professional in one's work, and not to be too pushy outside it – at least at first.

The other related consideration in terms of self-presentation is transparency. The US writer Ellen-Welsh (1995) suggests that in a rural setting, professionals cannot hide behind professional distance. Service users will value honesty and integrity and will appreciate the worker who acts in an authentically personal way – if they see a difference between the manner and conduct of the social worker within the working relationship, from what they might see in other settings in the community, credibility will be undermined. The example of the worker who is hard on alcohol consumption by the service user, but is a regular drinker in the local pub, is a notable one, as will be the worker whose personal relationships are complicated and gossip-worthy. There is nowhere to hide in the small rural community. Pugh (2000) discusses the notion of 'placing', whereby the rural service user, especially if they are an older person, will mean no disrespect in wanting to know enough personal information about the worker so that they will get some idea of who they are and to whom they might be related.

This would be unusual in the anonymity of an urban setting and would be viewed with suspicion by a worker, but in the rural dimension, this will help establish the worker's presence in the community.

Effective communication skills are involved in several of the requirements listed above. Martinez-Brawley (2000) explains that the rural and remotely based human services professional works at the point at which the horizontal systems of external policy makers meet the vertical reality of the community, and are often left to determine the application of such policies in an acceptable and user-friendly fashion. This requires particular communication and interpretation skills. There is also a question of meaning and its interpretation by the service user who has always lived in a remote area; Martinez-Brawley (2000) describes this as understanding and using 'high context' and 'low context' language. The social worker requiring information within set timescales for a written assessment will seek ready answers to prescribed questions in low context language. The answers might be given in a high context form, assuming knowledge of local customs, and shared knowledge and experience on the part of the listener. If such messages are not understood, valuable meaning can be lost and the worker will be left with an incomplete knowledge of their subject. The reduction of someone's life history to a series of dates and significant life events for a community care assessment illustrates this point – the service user might be perceived as going off in tangents in describing and emphasising events that have little meaning to the listener, whilst not providing the information required by the agency's form! This issue also pervades the minority and threatened language of Gaelic, lack of understanding of which might be a barrier to assessment in some Scottish island communities (Turbett, 2009a).

Remote and rural areas are generally ones with low levels of crime. The social worker going about their daily business is unlikely to have to worry about getting mugged, or having their vehicle stolen or vandalised. There are, however, particular safety issues as suggested in the final item on the list above. Service users often live in remote locations where help in the event of violence might be far away. Attention needs to be paid to proper risk assessment when predictable hazards are identified. This might be the possibility of physical harm from a service user with a mental health problem, or the repercussion of a confrontational interview over matters that have to be addressed with parents, such as child protection issues. Mobile telephones should be issued to staff and if they are out of range of signals, there is other technology available, including the AIRWAVE communication system used by the police and emergency services. Hazard may not stem from service user issues, but might arise from the remote and difficult-to-access location of their home, or weather conditions that can change suddenly and become lethal. Snow, icy back roads, exceptional rainfall bringing flooding, and gales that bring down trees and block roads, are all risks that should be discussed in the local context. The health and safety of staff is a corporate responsibility of employers but also a matter for which individuals themselves have to take some responsibility. Workers should not have to feel worried about raising such matters with supervisors.

Comfort in remote and rural settings: the work of Cheers, Darracott and Lonne

Most rurally based workers, especially those in the more remote settings, will recognise that whilst some are well suited to the environment, others do not settle and will probably move on quickly. The Australian writers Cheers, Darracott and Lonne (2005) have tried to make sense of the notion of how and why some workers achieve this and some do not, by developing a framework for examining the question based on a series of domains:

- the *society* domain (the grand narratives of the society and nation);
- the *structural* domain (the employing organisation and its political context);
- the *community* domain (the locality and its intersection with the wider community);

- the *geographic* domain (the geography and natural environment of the locality);
- the *personal* domain (the practitioner's personal, social and cultural background);
- the *professional* domain (knowledge, values, ethics, education and socialisation within the profession);
- The *practice fields* domain (eg dominant views on child protection);
- The *practice wisdom* domain (the practitioner's individual stage of expertise and development acquired through the reflexive channelling of skills, values and experience).

Cheers *et al.* suggest that whilst inconsistencies between domains are common in any setting, and can usually be accommodated (e.g. a society view that offenders should be punished versus an organizational and professional view that they should be helped), there will be some in rural practice that will lead to worker discomfort, stress and ill-health. The worker might feel caught between an organisational expectation that services are rationalised and provided according to eligibility criteria, and a community expectation that services should be there as of right: this can arise over admissions to residential care for older people (or conversely whether people should be able to remain in hospital and therefore are beyond charging policies applied for residential care). I was told of an incoming worker to a Gaelic-speaking community who would be shut out of discussions over particular personal issues in meetings, by a reversion to the minority language. That worker resolved to deal with the issue by learning the language.

A more obvious conflict or incongruity that relates to the worker's personal domain is whether they (and their family) can successfully reconcile the geographical remoteness and isolation, with their own need to shop, eat out, let off steam, go to premier league football matches, or simply be away from constant public scrutiny. Dealing with this may also involve other domains as the more reconciliation there is between them the more likely one is to resolve problematic areas within them. Thus, feeling comfortable about work in the sense of knowing what is expected by community members as well as being deliverable, along with a strong sense of connectedness with the community in its broadest sense, may balance out feelings of isolation.

The value of the domain concept is that it helps identify stressors and then helps examine if and how they might be resolved. It avoids disingenuous generalisations (and solutions) about problems that might be found and explains why, for some, the only answer to incongruity between domains will be to move on, whilst for others time and maturation into the job may resolve some difficulties experienced on first entering remote rural practice. I especially mention disingenuous solutions, as some agencies might be led through improper analysis to conclude that the only answer to the dilemmas of rural practice is to provide services from a distant location.

In this same paper, Cheers *et al.* state that the worker who settles into rural practice will experience the following:

- a community and geography with which they are connected and well suited;
- an organisation that provides defined direction, roles and support, yet allows autonomy to adjust policy and services to meet local needs, perspectives and aspirations;
- a position and practice field that matches their professional knowledge, skills and ethical morality;
- an integrated and reflexive orientation towards practice, development, and growth in their personal and professional domains.

These seem very reasonable and realisable aspirations, fitting within the roles and remits of Scottish social workers outlined earlier in this chapter.

Key summary points

■ Social workers use the same methods to address the same issues wherever they work, but rural communities present particular challenges, including difficulty of access to services.

■ Small communities present particular possibilities for community-orientated approaches, in terms of both community capacity building and working with individuals and families.

■ Even though there is a trend towards specialism, generalist skills are required as recognised in *Changing Lives.*

■ Rural workers require particular skills to negotiate the possibilities and pressures that arise from living and working within the one small community, including the particular issues arising from dual relationships and confidentiality. These require agency recognition, understanding and support.

■ The isolation of workers in all agencies nurtures mutual dependence and can lead to rewarding and good inter-agency working if properly focused.

■ Safety issues for remote and rurally based workers require special consideration. It should not be assumed that a rural environment is necessarily a safe one.

Recommended further reading

The chapter makes reference to most of the recent international texts on rural social work practice. Martinez-Brawley (the US) and Cheers (Australia) have published a considerable amount and any search will identify numerous journal papers written by other Canadian, US and Australian commentators. The UK literature is sparse, reflecting the absence of academic interest and teaching although Pugh has published a number of papers and the one principal UK reader. The following are especially recommended for their general relevance. The Pierson book is not specifically about rural practice but its generalist and community-orientated approach to social work resonates with the rural literature.

Ginsberg, L (ed) (1998) *Social Work in Rural Communities (3rd edition)*, Alexandria, VA: CSWE.

Lohmann, N and Lohmann, R (eds) (2005) *Rural Social Work Practice* New York: Columbia University Press.

Pierson, J (2008) *Going Local: Working in communities and neighbourhoods* London: Routledge.

Pugh, R (2000) *Rural Social Work* Lyme Regis, Russell House.

Pugh, R and Cheers, B (2010) *Rural Social Work: An international perspective* Bristol: The Policy Press.

Chapter 3

Childcare, Family Work and Child Protection

<hr>

Introduction

This chapter looks at problems and possibilities for good childcare work in rural and remote areas. First it looks at child protection, starting with an examination and analysis of two incidents in Scotland that have been drawn to public attention in recent years. The focus then moves on to discussion of case examples, and then on to the effect of male patriarchy in rural society. The chapter ends with discussion on work with young people in trouble.

Rural remote child protection: lessons from Orkney and Eilean Siar

In the past twenty years there have been a number of well-publicised child protection inquiries in Scotland with direct implications for professionals in rural and remote areas of the country. Two of these in particular, Orkney in 1991, and Eilean Siar (Western Isles) in 1995-2003, have thrown into sharp relief one of the central questions of this book: how, and indeed, whether, workers in rural and remote areas can keep ahead of the challenges presented by very complex situations unlikely to arise with any regularity in their practice. These inquiries will be examined with these issues in mind and further case studies will illustrate possibilities.

Both the Orkney Islands and Eilean Siar are sparsely populated remote-rural island communities on the very edge of Scotland. Orkney has a total population of 19,000 people with a population density of 19 people per square kilometre, and Eilean Siar has a population of 26,000 people with a density of nine people per square kilometre – respectively they have Scotland's smallest and third smallest local authorities. For comparison, the City of Edinburgh has 449,000 people with a density of 1,703 people per square kilometre and South Lanarkshire, with its mix of urban and rural communities, has 302,000 people with a density of 171 people per square kilometre (all figures from the 2001 National Census).

At dawn on 27 February 1991, Place of Safety Orders were used to remove, without warning, nine children from four family homes in the isolated community of South Ronaldsay in Orkney. The operation itself involved the police and experienced social workers brought in from as far away as Glasgow. The decision to do this was based on the accounts of children who had previously been removed from another family and who had been interviewed by specialist workers from an agency appointed by Orkney Islands Council. There were also perceptions around at that time that ritual abuse was a more widespread problem than had previously been imagined. These particular children were believed to have been subjected to sexual abuse with the collusion of their parents by a number of adults including a local church minister. In the end the allegations were robustly denied and a huge public outcry ensued: in the midst of international press interest, a sheriff at a Proof Hearing dropped the whole matter on procedural grounds. It was therefore never formally established whether there was any basis to the allegations (although the assumption generally since has been that there was none) and the children were all returned home. The ensuing public inquiry chaired by Lord Clyde was critical of just about everyone involved and its findings resulted in a major overhaul of childcare law in Scotland and the bringing onto the statute books of the Children (Scotland) Act 1995. Amongst many other things, the new legislation made it harder for social workers to remove children from their families without parental consent.

It has been argued elsewhere that the Orkney events were a lost opportunity for rural social work to put itself on the map as an effective specialism (Turbett, 2004). At the time, service delivery to remote communities was presented to the public inquiry as an issue, and included in its 191 findings (Clyde, 1992). The final finding suggested that Orkney Islands Council, particularly its Social Work Department, needed to improve its relationship with the communities it served. This was based on the comment in the inquiry report that not just all the families involved, but also almost all the staff involved, had migrated to Orkney from other parts of the UK. This scenario will be familiar to workers in remote rural communities where it is not uncommon for complex childcare cases to involve incomers who might have their own reasons for wanting to move to an isolated location, away, they perhaps perceive, from the scrutiny of authorities. The Clyde Report suggested that in the Orkney scenario indigenous locals were perhaps bewildered by outsiders who did not understand their community, delivering services to other outsiders and getting it all wrong.

Although the Eilean Siar situation had its differences from Orkney there were similarities. The children involved had moved into the community from elsewhere, but this time they came with a history of English social services involvement. The children's mother had a learning disability and had herself been sexually abused as a child, and she was believed herself to have abused other children. She already had a one-year-old daughter when in 1990 she married a convicted inter-familial sex offender and went on to have two more children with him. The family moved to Eilean Siar in 1995. The children were made subjects of Children's Hearing Supervision Orders in 1997 and by 2001 all had been removed from their parents' (or relatives') care and were being looked after by foster carers.

The official inquiry report identified that between 1990 and 2001 over 220 health concerns and allegations of physical, sexual and emotional abuse and neglect had been recorded through the interventions of over 100 professionals. Twelve child protection case conferences had been held in England and a further 17 in Eilean Siar, the children being on Child Protection Registers almost continuously, under the categories of at risk of sexual abuse, physical abuse and physical neglect (SWIA, 2005).

This time there seemed good reason to believe that the children involved had suffered abuse through the actions of a number of adults, although there was insufficient evidence to bring the nine adults charged (after a dawn police operation) in 2003 to prosecution. Attention was focused not on why social workers did what they did, but given their active involvement, why they and colleagues in partner agencies had not read the signs of abuse effectively so that they might have acted to protect the children at a much earlier date. As with Orkney, there was criticism of the absence of proper evaluation and assessment of the information known to the principal agencies, and a recommendation that shared chronologies of significant events should be introduced, was prominent in the report. Other criticisms concerned the *rule of optimism* (whereby workers feel that they must be making a difference and look for evidence of that rather than seeing the objective reality), and the emphasis being on parental support rather than a focus on the needs of the children. These are not uncommon features of child protection inquiries, the Jasmine Beckford report (London Borough of Brent, 2005) being the first to quote the importance of such factors.

As echoed in earlier inquiries, concern was expressed that assessments had focused on the perceived co-operation of parents rather than on measurable changes for the children. Most inquiries surrounding matters of major public and professional concern, of course, relate to children in urban areas.

There were also issues about the deficit in resources in Eilean Siar. A dearth of foster carers mean that the removal of the children would necessarily mean placing them some distance away from family, friends and home community. This of course was a particular criticism of the Orkney situation when children were deliberately removed to situations on the Scottish mainland where they were deemed to be safe because of such distance.

The quality of supervision available to social work staff was considered in the Eilean Siar inquiry report. In the report (SWIA, 2005) there was criticism that although supervision discussion about the family was systematic, it was always focused on current concerns and failed to adequately review developments over a period of time. There was similarly criticism of the inadequacy of quality assurance on child protection work by social work managers, and the arrangements for chairing child protection case conferences and looked-after children reviews. Training and supervision were given substantial coverage in the influential report into the death of Victoria Climbié in London in February 2000 (Laming, 2003, Recommendations 31, 37, 45 and 52); workload management/time availability is also regarded as a significant factor in enabling workers to perform reasonably (e.g. Hawthorn, 2009, Recommendation 11.9, to quote a Scottish example).

Both the Orkney and Eilean Siar inquiries referred to social workers working beyond their own levels of competence. In Orkney, Lord Clyde recommended the creation of 'a central resource … to provide a high level of expertise for guidance, advice and support in particular cases where such assistance may be of support (Clyde, 1992, Recommendation 33). The Eilean Siar report stated: 'the professionals working with family A lacked the necessary expertise to effectively protect the children. We question whether an area such as Eilean Siar can ever have the range of expertise to address such complex child abuse issues' (Social Work Inspection Agency, 2005, p. 78). Again here the reports echo one another, Lord Clyde stated: 'The whole area of work in child protection requires to be seen as a specialist area to be undertaken by practitioners with specialist skills and knowledge with adequate training and support' (Clyde, 1992, Recommendation 173). The Eilean Siar inquiry discussed comments made within the profession after the Orkney events but interestingly stated that 'it is likely that *all* authorities will require access to some external expert for staff working with complex child protection cases' (SWIA, 2005, p. 79, emphasis added). The report made this one of its recommendations just as Lord Clyde had also called for a similar central resource in 1992. There seems evidence, based on the findings of the Climbié report referred to above, that training and the absence of an 'expert' are issues irrespective of location.

It therefore seems that despite some inference that workers in these remote areas were poor country cousins when it came to their approach to the needs of children in complex child protection cases, the evidence rather suggests that they were prey to the same pitfalls and problems as their urban colleagues. It is contended here that with adequate training (including formal post-graduate training such as the Diploma Courses in Child Protection run by a number of Scottish universities), and a Scottish-based resource back-up as suggested by Lord Clyde and the Social Work Inspection Agency (SWIA) in their respective inquiry reports (and recently implemented with the creation of the Multi Agency Resource Service – MARS – based at Stirling University), practice in rural and remote areas can be as cutting edge as anywhere else. The strengths brought by locally based workers can, in fact, enhance child protection. Let us now look at some practice illustrations.

Children and family case examples

- The **A family** move into a substandard rented house in a remote island location from the North of England. They immediately begin making demands on services, explaining that in their previous council tenancy in an urban area they suffered harassment from neighbours and little help from the authorities. There are two school-age children in the family who have health problems and disabilities, although the nature of these is not obvious and only partially reflected in the records that eventually come from education and health sources in their former area. Another two-year-old child is said by the mother to be showing similar signs of 'attention deficit disorder'. The family have moved to make a fresh start in a better environment, one of the adults having enjoyed holidays on the island in their childhood. Demands made are so insistent that social work attention is made available on the basis that further assessment is required to explore the needs of the children and how they are being met within the family and elsewhere.

- The **B family**, who have two children aged 9 and 12, move into a remotely located private tenancy several miles from the nearest habitation. The mother is pregnant and comes to the attention of the local general practitioner (GP) and is referred to the midwife. She is concerned by a number of things: the family seem to have changed their name, there is a big age difference between the older father and the mother, they seem to have had regular changes of address all over the UK and they seem to lead a very insular way of life: the last of these is characterised by very fundamental Christian beliefs and home education of the children. The parents are resistant to inquiry and highly suspicious. The GP and midwife contact social services for some discussion and advice.

- The **C family** consist of the parents, who were born and bred in the small village where they live and their one pre-school and two primary school age children. The father has a past history of alcohol abuse that has resulted in a criminal record for violent offences when he was a young man. The mother is a highly strung individual who spends most of her day watching daytime television, adopting many of the traits of the characters she sees in reality and soap shows. Neither of the couple enjoys significant positive extended family support, family history suggesting that both grew up in situations where alcohol abuse and poverty were accepted features of life. Demands are frequently made on social services to intervene in family quarrels or 'sort out' one or other child. The family also regularly encounter financial crisis as neither parent works for 'health' reasons. The primary school is concerned about the behaviour of the children at school and believes this reflects dynamics at home.

These are all typical scenarios drawn from real life, characterising the type of work that comes to social workers who serve remote rural locations. The first two contain the type of summarised information that would be available early on in the life of a new referral, whilst the C family are likely to have records and even past assessments available. None of the referrals suggests that children are at immediate risk of harm, let alone significant harm, but all would probably ring alarm bells with social workers. The purpose of the following is not to analyse such referrals for child protection purposes but to draw out the particularities and peculiarities of rural practice possibilities. In comparison with social workers that might be faced with similar scenarios in an urban situation, the rural worker will have strengths and advantages to bring to assessment and intervention:

- the possibility of personal knowledge of family and individuals involved (C family);
- a close working relationship with other key agencies: community health staff and GP, headteacher and other school staff, the police (all three families);
- a realistic working knowledge of community resources that might be called on to support family members, for example housing, childcare support, parenting help, youth facilities (all three families);
- an understanding of the networking possibilities – both positive and negative – available in the community that might either increase risk and vulnerability, or help reduce it (all three families), for example the type of neighbourhood they live in and what support might be possible from neighbours; and physical isolation factors such as public transport availability (all three families).

Watkins (2004, p. 67) states: 'The interconnectedness of rural resources provides a helping environment very different from the formality of the urban network'. What he describes is how the separate networks that link individuals, their families, neighbours and the various formal helping services that might be available, are likely to connect directly in a rural community. This arises from the general knowledge that people in rural remote areas have of their own communities, and the natural ties that they have with each other. Martinez-Brawley (2000) adds to this by suggesting that social workers in rural communities lie at the meeting point between the horizontal links that community members have with each other, and the vertical links that communities have with agencies that make policy and deliver services from the outside:

'Social workers face concrete problems that carry the unique mark of the community in which they arise. They need to be as interested in the horizontal ties binding community members as in the vertical ties connecting professionals with the social provisions they interpret'
(Martinez-Brawley, 2000, p. 80).

This has the potential for the development of trust and identity with the agency that is simply missing in an urban setting.

Using this model, **Family C** might see social services as an understood and familiar local helping agency, rather than an outside threat. The parents might agree to accept help with their parenting skills: in a rural community it is unlikely that parenting classes would be immediately available, but a generalist social worker (see Chapter 2) will make it their business to facilitate the establishment of such a resource, and might be involved directly in its delivery. Family C may be familiar with workers from their sharing of the same small community space: their children may attend the same schools and they will use the same shops. The issue of dual relationships that arise was discussed in Chapter 2. What will be important for the maintenance of a credible professional relationship, is that the worker enjoys a general respect in the community and is not the subject of gossip – a factor that can prove very undermining. A family who have a history of alcohol problems themselves will not be helped by a worker known to drink heavily in a local hostelry. If the nature of the dual relationship between potential worker and service user is problematic for any reason then consideration must be given to this in the allocation process (Johnson, 2009, p. 55). When workers work to a generalist model in a rural setting, there is also a need to consider the requirement to separate responsibilities for needy parents (e.g. who have addiction issues) with their own agendas, from their children whose needs have to be separately assessed and given paramount consideration. As seen in the Victoria Climbié and other inquiry cases (including Eilean Siar), some parents have a skilled ability to deflect workers' attention from their children's real needs to their own. In a rural area the consequent allocation of two social workers to one family might have serious resource implications, but is a consideration of primary importance.

Rural workers will recognise and work with social diversity: disadvantaged families will live amongst those who are better off and care needs to be taken not to stigmatise children and their parents such as those from Family C. Services that provide support may have to be tailored to the needs of a scattered population. The Sure Start initiative provides a good opportunity for innovative work in this respect: funding could be made available for whatever fitted best – outreach or mobile services, or transport to get children to early years provision (The Countryside Agency, 2003). It is to be hoped that the crisis in public sector funding identified in Chapter 1 does not end all this.

Family B might be enabled to see agencies that take an interest in their affairs as helping and supportive rather than threatening and intrusive. In this way there might be success in helping them settle where they are, rather than feel pressured to move on. Although cities almost certainly offer more anonymity than rural locations, the anecdotal experience of rural workers would suggest that some types of family believe that escape from conformity and even anonymity are to be found by moving to remote rural areas, when the opposite will be the actual experience found (Martinez-Brawley, 2000). Dealing with Christian religious fundamentalist attitudes requires particular skills from the rural worker: Denton and Denton (1998, p. 160), from an

American perspective where this is commonly encountered, suggest that workers should be conscious of their own belief system and biases, and that they require specific knowledge and use of 'belief congruent techniques' in order to effectively enter the worlds of such families. Horwarth and Lees (2010) suggest that the effect of religious beliefs and values on family life have to be taken into account when assessing children in need. Values such as Biblical-based patriarchy have to be approached carefully (see below). Families such as Family B certainly offer challenges to those professionals required to assess the situations of their children: a balance needing to be struck between the human rights of the parents (e.g. cultural diversity and religious belief) and the rights and needs of children, particularly for protection from harm. The difficulties in achieving this balance lie at the heart of child protection work and underpin effective risk assessment (Munro, 2002, pp. 87, 105). It will be as hard to achieve in a rural area as in a culturally and ethnically diverse urban one. Major considerations in equipping workers and teams to deal with such matters are training, supervision and workload management. These are issues, as mentioned earlier in this chapter in relation to the Eilean Siar inquiry, which feature prominently in a number of child protection inquiries in urban areas where cultural and ethnic diversity are commonplace.

Family A might be encouraged to adopt a more realistic perspective of their own situation and what they might expect of helping agencies in the locality. This will be of more benefit to the children than conflict with agencies stemming from demands by the parents perceived as unreasonable. Knowledge of community resources might act as a bridge between the family and the networks that might help them. Careful negotiation over roles between agencies used to working closely together will help bolster their respective roles and enhance the support to the children concerned. This is consistent with GIRFEC principles – the partnership working for the benefit of children encouraged in official Scottish Executive reports: *Getting It Right for Every Child* (Scottish Executive, 2005) and *It's Everyone's Job to Make Sure I'm Alright* (Scottish Executive, 2002). Such principles are perhaps easier to action in isolated communities than in urban ones where agency structures are complex and working relationships difficult to foster because of staff turnover. As commented elsewhere, workers from different agencies co-operate well together in remote settings when they are mutually dependent and therefore feel part of the same team (Turbett, 2004, p. 988).

Patriarchy, 'macho' culture and domestic abuse in rural areas

Feminist-inspired critiques of social work practice have been a feature of the profession for the last twenty years or more 'whilst never fully hitting the mainstream of social work education or practice' (Ferguson and Woodward, 2009, p. 25). However, such influences drive the work of Women's Aid, the principal voluntary organisation supporting women and children who suffer domestic abuse in Scotland, and ideas about the non-acceptability of violence between the adult partners within family settings (usually perpetrated by men towards women) also drive police and judicial responses.

From the Canadian experience, Tranter (2005, p. 105) suggests that patriarchy, male dominance (and masculinity) are common features in rural settings. Mermelstein (1991) writes of this in US farming communities suffering from economic decay. She found that whilst men suffered shame and guilt through their loss of status, resulting in high suicide rates (a fact also recorded in UK farming communities facing decline), the women were better motivated to save their communities and fight for the future, rather like the miners' wives during the 1984-85 strike in the UK. Pugh and Cheers (2010) confirm the rural prevalence of patriarchy from their review of research internationally and link this to the nature of agricultural work in small farm units. Evidence from UK research shows that women in rural communities are disadvantaged, in terms of employment and income, education, participation in civic activity, culture and aspiration (Commission for Rural Communities, 2006). Despite measured progress and legal attempts to provide remedies, gender inequality remains a feature of Scottish society (Breitenbach and Wassof, 2007), and might be expected in remote and rural areas where traditional values regarding gender roles have prevailed. Whilst Tranter's research concerned isolated, hard-living and hard-working single-industry towns in the Canadian North, the cultures of other types of isolated community are not so different when it comes to masculinity and its features, and their impact on family life. One difference might be that religion and tradition still hold some sway in isolated Scottish communities where outward migration is a problem, but might be absent as an influence in areas of recent inward migration in Canada. However, in the Western Isles of Scotland, the very heart of vibrant Presbyterianism, the significance of gender difference can be evidenced by reference to available information on alcohol-related deaths: whilst that amongst men is amongst the highest in Scotland, that amongst women, in contrast, is amongst the lowest (NHS Scotland, 2009). High suicide rates amongst young men in the Highlands of Scotland have also been associated with 'macho' and 'laddish' culture (BBC News Scotland, 1999).

The breakdown of traditional values and family networks is linked in the popular imagination with child abuse (see Grayling, 2008, for a balanced discussion on such notions) but such beliefs do not explain the prevalence of abusive relationships in rural areas; however, a breakdown of community cohesiveness and strength perhaps offers a better explanation (Joseph Rowntree Foundation, 2009, p. 16). In 2002, I visited an isolated area of Western Newfoundland in Canada where relatively widespread inter-familial sexual abuse had been 'discovered' within fairly recent times in a community suffering from decline and depopulation (Turbett, 2006).

Issues concerning the invisibility of powerful male figures responsible for harm in family settings have been explored in feminist-inspired social work literature (Valentich, 1996; Scoursfield, 2003), and are deserving of attention within a profession that still focuses heavily on women (often themselves victims) and their responsibilities for the protection of children. There is a particular danger of this in rural settings where working fathers may be employed away from home due to the absence of work opportunity locally. A recent national survey conducted for the National Federation of Women's Institutes (NFWI) on violence against women in UK urban and rural settings, identified that perpetrator programmes are the least accessible of all services dealing with the issues (McCarry and Williamson, 2009, p. 36); a pilot project for perpetrators placed on probation in Edinburgh will go some way to addressing this shortfall if rolled out to Criminal Justice Services elsewhere in Scotland (Scottish Government, 2009k). The NFWI survey also identified that in rural areas women respondents were more likely to consider that women could do more to avoid being victims, another factor that removes responsibility from male perpetrators (McCarry and Williamson, 2009, p. 16) and that they are less likely to consider gender inequality as a root cause of male violence towards women. This is supported by Wendt and Cheers' (2002, p. 29) Australian research which reported victims saying that friends and family would ignore the reality of domestic violence, and if confronted with it, would 'walk away': 'People in the standard, happy marriage are very judgmental' said one respondent.

Women suffering abuse may be trapped in the home due to the absence of alternative opportunity (e.g. for housing) in their home areas where there are at least some informal supports from friends and family (Pugh, 2000, p. 141). Fleeing domestic abuse will usually involve uprooting children from school and friends and a move far away to a very different urban environment (Save the Children, 2003, pp. 25, 52). My own professional experience locally suggests that Women's Aid in Scotland has a good appreciation of rural factors. Domestic abuse remains a 'hidden issue' in rural areas for social and economic reasons, underlined by the NFWI survey which demonstrated that whilst figures were similar for both rural and urban areas, rural dwellers were less likely to perceive it as an issue within their communities (McCarry and Williamson, 2009). Rural women are reported to be more likely to migrate elsewhere than rural men (Pugh and Cheers, 2010); we can presume that escape for women from restriction of personal opportunity might be a reason for consequent gender imbalance in some rural communities characterised by patriarchy.

Social workers should be prepared to confront and challenge patriarchy and a 'macho' culture in rural areas because of all the evidence of the damage and harm that underlie such values (Wendt and Cheers, 2002). In Chapter 2 it was suggested that in the early stages of fitting into a rural practice setting, it might be best to maintain a low profile. This advice will probably apply to public challenges to patriarchy if this is endemic and accepted within a community – more lasting impact will be made by the worker who has earned some acceptance and respect. This does not imply turning a blind eye to injustice within families or refusing to seek empowerment of oppressed women. Challenge will not be an easy task and traits of patriarchy may even be found within employing organisations. Wendt (2010) argues that differences in understanding of domestic abuse and family violence amongst workers in a rural Australian setting had the potential to impede an effective and coordinated response. The following checklist is offered for consideration by all social workers who work with families:

- Does the culture of your workplace and employing organisation challenge or support patriarchy?
- Is domestic abuse considered an issue in the locality where you work – if not why not?
- What steps can you take to challenge male hegemony within the families you work with?
- When considering child protection issues within a family, are the male figures receiving an appropriate level of attention, or is the focus on the mother figure as protector?

All of these questions (and there are many more), imply action by workers, individually and collectively. Too often such issues are seen as urban ones when the reality is that rural settings are the ones where particular attention may be required to issues of patriarchy and a macho culture.

Working with young people in trouble

It is important when considering the issues surrounding work with troubled young people in rural areas to begin by considering where young people fit within the wider social context of their localities. Rural areas are generally considered ideal places to grow up and this is often quoted as a reason families choose to live in them. Glendinning *et al.* (2003) found that whilst living in rural communities was linked with wellbeing for adults and young children, there was less evidence when it came to teenagers and young people. Shucksmith's review of research into social exclusion in rural areas contains the following insightful passage that will be recognised by many:

> David and Ridge (1997) argue that "in rural areas, children and young people find themselves in a very particular social environment where there may be powerful adult groups (affluent incomers and early retirers seeking an idyllic rural lifestyle) who can dominate in a struggle for space and resources; where children and young people can be very visible yet find their needs both invisible and unmet." For those on a low income, these effects are heightened. Often there is a lack of space for young people within their own communities. "One of the consequences of the lack of sanctioned space to play and congregate is that children and young people become highly visible in their communities, and subject to adult scrutiny and in many cases disapproval. This can result in a situation whereby children and young people are seen as a problem rather than as contributory members of their communities."
>
> (Shucksmith, 2003, p. 15)

Bailey *et al.* (2004) echo this in their report on social exclusion in Argyll and Bute, remarking that in Campbeltown (a remote town on the Kintyre peninsula), large numbers of young people gather in public places, causing friction with authority and a poor relationship with the wider community. A study in Cornwall in England found the same thing and considered that this seems to be linked with an absence of meeting places and amenities for young people in rural areas (Howard League for Penal Reform, 2005). The authors noted that unlike urban areas of deprivation where people affected were grouped together in particular areas, the socially deprived in rural areas tended to be scattered amongst the rest of the population and were therefore encroaching on contested space. They went on to suggest that the use of Anti-Social Behaviour Orders (ASBOs) to resolve such issues had further excluded young people in rural communities and called for the inclusion of young people in projects to improve provision and promote more positive relationships with other groups. The use of ASBOs in Scotland under the terms of the Anti-Social Behaviour (Scotland) Act 2004, is not without controversy. Their use effectively undermines the welfare principle that pervades all other Scottish law and policy relating to children and young people (Hothersall, 2008), removes basic rights from children and parents, and allows for direct referral to a Sheriff Court on the basis of evidence that requires little in the way of legal proof. The fact that this was championed by a Scottish Executive Labour Minister, Cathy Jamieson MSP, who had previously worked as a children's rights advocate in Ayrshire, suggests the extent to which this agenda was driven by popular politics rather than sound principle.

Alcohol abuse is recognised by government as being a huge issue in Scottish society (Scottish Government, 2009j), and steps have been taken to try to make it harder for young people to access drink. This includes measures such as encouraging retailers to ask for proof of age when selling alcohol, and restricting sales to particular areas of shops. In rural areas there can be complacency about alcohol use by adults (including parents) that stems from cultural norms and a belief that if young people are drinking then at least they are not using illegal drugs. Social workers alongside other agencies in rural communities have a responsibility to challenge such assumptions and help parents assume a proper responsibility for their children. Only then can those few young people who are at genuine risk from addiction problems be better identified and helped.

Children and young people in trouble across Scotland typically encounter a myriad range of social work and youth justice services. They will often be assessed by a council-employed social worker from a specialist assessment team, but if placed on a Supervision Order may be referred to a project in the voluntary/not-for-profit sector. This might involve groupwork, individual mentoring, intensive support round the clock, skills-based training, outdoor activities, reparative justice work, family group conferencing – the list is a long one and will vary from area to area. Providers change as contracts are won and lost according to the *Best Value* principles of local government. As discussed above, persistent offenders and their parents may also find themselves subject to more punitive approaches under ASBO systems.

In cities and urban areas there may be a choice about what is the best resource for a young person. However, in rural and remote communities, there may be few if any resources within easy distance and escalation up the tariff to removal from home can follow a young person whose issues seem intransigent. Children and family social workers will need to be innovative and resourceful in the best traditions of the generalist model described in Chapter 2. Sometimes this can involve the development of resources as need arises: in remote areas there may not always be sufficient demand to justify permanently staffed specialised projects. In North Ayrshire a centrally located individual mentoring project within social services facilitates the employment of sessionally employed mentors who can be recruited wherever and whenever need arises. This can involve individuals with time and skills (perhaps the young retired) to spend usefully with otherwise marginalised young people, and can help address the problem of social exclusion referred to at the start of this section. Mentoring projects have been widely evaluated (Philip *et al.*, 2004) and lend themselves particularly well to remote rural situations. They do not, however, run themselves, and mentors require good support and supervision if their efforts are to be effective.

It may be possible to develop resources that can be used flexibly across wide areas. An example of an innovative rural project was demonstrated by the Perth and Kinross Rural Youth Project whose activities between 1989 and 1994 were evaluated and reported (Kendrick and Rioch, 1995). This project, run by NCH Action for Children across the large rural hinterlands of Tayside Region (an area of over 2,000 square miles with a population of over 82,000 people), organised principally around groupwork, also involved individual work, and in most cases work with parents. 'Highly structured' groupwork programmes of approximately ten-week duration were run in a number of locations across the area, using a "social skills approach" to develop 'self control and social responsibility'. The results were impressive: the majority were referred on an early intervention basis before they became subjects of statutory intervention, for reasons ranging from poor school behaviour and attendance, through to offending. In 64 per cent of all cases (72 per cent in the case of those referred for offending), positive outcomes were reported. It is perhaps indicative of the time that the paper on this project was written that it provides no information on costs. However, it must be assumed that even if a few young people were diverted from residential school placement (with costs per young person currently averaging several thousand pounds per week), the project showed cost effectiveness.

Community-orientated early-intervention approaches were reported by Green (1989, 1993) in descriptions of the work of the Badenoch and Strathspey Team in the Highland Region in the 1980s. The team reflected on the volume of children they were being asked by Children's Hearings to look after and accommodate because of issues such as chronic school attendance and family dysfunction, all of which were resulting in school exclusion. A proactive approach was taken to open up communication with teachers and health colleagues, help their understanding of the social problems of the children they were encountering, and reintegrate the children into schools and the broader community. This ran alongside early identification through such dialogue of children who had problems and the offer of effective support in a variety of ways to their families. This resulted in a reduction in looked-after children and 'containment' of the statutory caseload, to the extent resources allocation suffered (Green, 1989, p. 119).

Reading Green some twenty years later it is clear that broader policy initiatives in the UK have caught up with the innovatory practice of his team; in Scotland the GIRFEC framework (referred to earlier in this chapter) is supposed to ensure such dialogue and practice. One of Green's points though was that distance and resource scarcity in rural areas engendered the sensible sharing of information and resources, and social workers were uniquely placed to promote these things. That message remains as true today across all areas of social work activity, and especially in dealing with excluded young people. To paraphrase Martinez-Brawley (2000) whose ideas were discussed in Chapter 2, rural social workers lie at the confluence of government policy and local community and will be subject to tensions and expectations from both directions. On the one hand, they have to work within a system that might centrally provide direction and strategy (and funding or non-funding) that conflicts with local aspirations; and on the other hand, they are living and working alongside community members who can be personally and volubly critical if services are not as they would wish them to be.

Key summary points

■ Despite assertions to the contrary, there is no evidence to suggest that with effective training and support, rural and remotely based social workers are not as able to deal with complex child protection issues as their urban colleagues.

■ The mutual inter-dependence characteristic of rural and remote locations can foster good inter-agency practice in child protection. This fits well with the GIRFEC Agenda in Scotland.

■ Patriarchy is a common feature in families in rural areas and requires appreciation of its consequences, and action by workers individually and collectively. It is not just damaging to women, but men also. Remote and rural areas are difficult environments, for many reasons, for women to escape domestic abuse.

■ Young people can find themselves particularly socially excluded and marginalised in rural areas where dominant influence is often held by affluent groups whose members have little sympathy for their situations. However, these same groups may have people with the time and skills to make a difference to the lives of young people.

■ Resource creation to divert young people from anti-social activity in remote rural areas requires flexibility and inventiveness.

Recommended further reading

There is a dearth of literature specific to children and family work in the rural literature, tending as it does to be generalist in nature, and a list of the most useful of these is given at the end of Chapter 2. However, the Canadian text below is of interest, touching on many of the themes in this chapter. The two inquiry reports are essential reference points for the Scottish context. The Howard League for Penal Reform pamphlet summarises useful and relevant research concerning young people in trouble.

Brownlee, K and Graham, J (eds) (2005) *Violence in the Family: Social work readings and research from Northern and rural Canada* Toronto: CSPI.

Clyde, Lord (1992) *The Report of the Inquiry into the Removal of Children from Orkney in February 1991* Edinburgh: HMSO.

Howard League for Penal Reform (2005) *Once Upon a Time in the West: Social deprivation and rural youth crime* London: Howard League for Penal Reform.

Social Work Inspection Agency (2005) *An Inspection into the Care and Protection of Children in Eilean Siar* Edinburgh: Scottish Executive.

Chapter 4

Working with Adults

Introduction

This chapter looks at debates and issues surrounding social work with adults in Scotland within the context of remote and rural communities. It begins with an examination of community care policy and practice, including critical discussion of the Personalisation Agenda that now seems crucial for future developments. It goes on to look briefly at criminal justice work in the remote and rural context. Finally, by way of historical digression, it looks at the past practice of boarding out adults with learning disabilities to farms in rural Scotland.

Community care in Scotland: an overview

The NHS and Community Care Act 1990 encapsulated a shift in social policy that had been happening for many years. Whilst 'community care' was not introduced by statute, the formalisation of this as policy following the 1988 publication of the Griffiths Report made it an aspiration that was now central to welfare policy (Barnes, 1997). Local authority social work with adults has since been largely determined by formal assessment of need and consequent management of service delivery. As the policy has developed, the emphasis has increasingly been on resource rationing within frameworks that talk about user choice and empowerment – a process fraught with dilemma and contradiction (Barnes, 1997, p. 95). The task of social workers is to assess and care manage using prescribed formats, with little time to form the helping relationships with individuals that have always been regarded as fundamental to casework (Ferguson and Woodward, 2009). The term 'community care', used generically to describe services to adults, has been described as:

> ... a distinctive range of professional practice ... some people's everyday experience of life, the inspiration of a movement away from institutional care and towards supported life in the community, a euphemism for women's labour in the home, and the focus for intense debate and controversy.
>
> (Bornat et al., 1993, p. xi)

Taking such variations into account, this chapter will focus on the actuality and potential within remote and rural communities for social work practice that lies within the parameters set by employers, and by government policy. In the past most social work interventions with vulnerable adults were dealt with in institutional settings, often, but not always, using a health rather than a social model: hospitals for what were regarded as chronic conditions (including physical and learning disabilities), psychiatric hospitals and residential care homes. All of these still exist but policy within the context of 'community care' has been to deal with people wherever possible within community settings. Whilst the policy driver contained a strong element of the need to reduce expense, few would argue that large institutions were, for many people, devoid of opportunity for quality of life, independence and individuality. However, under the guise of offering choice and provision of service according to need, the community care reforms introduced a business model into social work, with a market for services, and recipients being cast in the role of customers (Harris, 2003). This model applies generally to social work with older people, adults with physical disabilities, those with chronic health conditions, adults with learning disabilities, adults with mental health problems and those with addiction problems.

Quality is assured through the Regulation of Care (Scotland) Act 2000, with inspection regimes enforcing national care standards on services and Codes of Practice for individually registered staff. Charges are often made on service users, usually based on some type of means testing. The exception to the latter rule, unique just now to the Scottish social care scene, is the concept of 'free personal care' for people over the age of 65 years. Under this scheme, personal care (a set list of tasks including washing, assistance with feeding and dressing, but excluding cleaning and shopping) is provided free to people requiring such help within their own homes. In residential settings a fixed sum is given to those whose personal capital is over a certain limit (currently £21,500) to cover the cost of the care element of their weekly bill, but they pay the balance – the 'hotel charge' covering the cost of their bed and board. Not unnaturally, the scheme is popular with those in the population who have been able to save during their working lives, or who own property (although hotel charges will eat into such savings over time, and property may still have to be sold). For poorer members of the community, free personal care means little. The scheme, however, costs £101 million per year (BBC News, 2009) and, given the pressures on the public purse and the increase in the older population, referred to in Chapter 1, may not survive in its present form.

Resource scarcity and poor access to services are associated with remote and rural areas: both become bigger issues the further one moves down the urban-rural continuum (Pugh et al., 2007). This inevitably results in tensions with the agenda described above. Choice within a market framework is unlikely to exist in a rural area, and indeed some aspects of the marketplace may not exist at all. These and other issues relating to the practice as discussed in Chapter 2, will both restrict and extend possibilities for good community care in rural and remote areas in Scotland.

The Personalisation Agenda

The principal policy driver across social care, and prominently featuring in discussion on developing community-based services for adults, is *personalisation.* The need for more individualisation and choice has been around since the early 1990s, with pressure from the disabled users movement eventually resulting in the introduction of Direct Payments by the end of the decade (Barnes, 1997). Personalisation emerged from DEMOS, a New Labour think tank, in 2004 (Leadbeater, 2004) and has since entered the Scottish arena as a strand of the *Changing Lives* review of social work (Scottish Executive, 2006), and is now a central policy plank (Scottish Government, 2009h). Personalisation is in some respects an extension of the policy of Direct Payments: this enables service users to opt to take cash in lieu of services to meet needs assessed by professionals (usually social workers) so that they can commission their own services from an independent provider or employ their own staff. Direct Payments take-up in Scotland has been low and in 2008 only numbered a few thousand individual cases (Scottish Government, 2008). However personalisation takes matters beyond the allocation of individualised budgets and is, in the words of its architects, 'not a set of policies but a general approach to public services and social care that puts the person at the centre as a participant in shaping the services they get, managing risk and providing resources, whether financial or in terms of their own effort' (Leadbeater and Lownsbrough, 2005, p.25).

The goal of personalisation is held up as a liberating process for both service users and social workers. The former will change from being 'consumers of public services ... to participants and investors in their own care'. The latter, currently working within a profession riddled with 'cynicism, disaffection and demoralisation', will be 'reconnected with the goals and values underpinning the profession' (Leadbeater and Lownsbrough, 2005, p. 4). This will be achieved by changing the way social care is funded, organised and staffed (2005, p. 32). Such changes are required because of increasing expectations amongst 'customers' [*sic*], the need to change the emphasis from 'inputs and process ... to outcomes', and find 'cost, as well as person, effective solutions' (Scottish Government, 2009h, p. 11). A step process for personalised commissioning is suggested involving information giving, individual support and advocacy, self-assessment, individual budgets, support planning and support choice and control (Scottish Government, 2009h, p. 11). A strong emphasis is put on the enabling of support on a preventative level through communities and within families, and recognition given that this will require investment as well as a shift away from the provision of expensive resources at the critical pinnacle of the triangle when a minority of individuals are in crisis. This fits with the need to shift the balance of care within a context, as described in Chapter 1, where need, especially within the ageing population, will soon outstrip available resources. Change will be required in the way communities see themselves and how they can look after their own, and how they and their individual members relate to the state. Change will also be required of the workforce: the role of the social worker will move away from assessment and care management to that of advisor, navigator, broker, service provider, risk assessor and auditor (in more complex cases) and 'designers of the social care system to help draw together formal, informal, voluntary and private sector care providers' (Leadbeater and Lownsbrough, 2005, p. 37). Those opposed to such changes are characterised as 'barriers' who are fearful of change, with an interest in the status quo, or 'reluctant to accept that services may have to be de-commissioned' (Scottish Government, 2009h, p. 44).

In the rural context personalisation is considered to perhaps provide an answer to rural service delivery gaps and problems. Soon after the introduction of old-age pensions by the Liberal Government in 1911, the writer Neil Munro put the possibilities that this new funding stream created for enterprising island farmers into the mouth of his kenspeckle character Para Handy, skipper of the puffer 'Vital Spark'. In the tale 'Pension Farms', Para Handy recounted how friends of his on Mull and Gigha were collecting pensioners and 'farming' them to gain the rewards of their state incomes:

When my frien collected them, they hadna what you would caal an object for to live for except it was their own funeral; noo they're daft

for almanacs, and makin plans for living to a hundred when the fermer
tells them he'll gie them each a medal and a uniform.

(Munro, 1942, p. 147)

This comic-fiction century-old suggestion for the exploitation of older people for financial gain, but at the same time offering a quality of life that might not otherwise be available, echoes down the years to our own time. The reader can decide what this might tell us about the agendas we work with today!

On the basis of a reported high number of Direct Payment cases in Orkney, Leadbeater and Lownsbrough (2005, p. 47) argue that 'the dispersal of the rural population and the difficulty of reaching it with traditional services may make the case for personalisation stronger'. This is rather a quantum leap: throughout rural Scotland efforts have been made to provide imaginative services that bring people together to share services on the type of cost-and-person effective basis that they advocate. This is true in the Western Isles and elsewhere for daycare resources for various service user groups, including people with learning disabilities, frail older people and people with dementia. However, an emphasis on individual budgets and opting out of such services in order to invent a personal support package, will inevitably have a 'critical mass' effect (Smith and Homer, 2009) and threaten the future of such collective services.

In their study on the potential impact of personalisation policies in the countryside, Manthorpe and Stevens (2009) urged caution, suggesting that monitoring is required to ensure that there really are equitable outcomes for rural areas and that promises are fulfilled. However, they reported that service users and others all commented that choice and control were lacking within current systems, and that services imposed as a result of assessment were devoid of flexibility. One respondent commented that personalised budgets might enable care and support to be 'more sympathetic to rural life' and delivered by care workers who understood rural communities (2009, p. 8).

Whether such aspirations can be delivered through personalisation is, as

Manthorpe and Stevens commented, the crucial question. In rural locations such as North Ayrshire, recruitment problems for local authority homecare staff have been overcome by proper contracted employment on a fixed basis rather than zero-hour casual employment. This has improved the consistency of service by encouraging staff retention through reasonable pay and service conditions, and the benefits of a well-trained and experienced workforce recruited locally. Individualised budgets and the broadening of direct payment systems have the potential to threaten the future of these hard-won service improvements. The vision of the creation of agency or user-employed support posts as an alternative to present local authority service arrangements conjures up the very image that the government service development group looking at the issue say they want to avoid: that of services being provided by casualised low-paid women and migrant workers (Scottish Government, 2009h). This is certainly a concern of UNISON, the trade union that represents large sections of the social care workforce, there being a very real fear that choice will be promoted at the expense of broader welfare (UNISON, 2009). An example it gives is that of local authorities that have replaced delivered meals-on-wheels services (which involve human contact) with a choice of companies that provide a month's worth of microwaveable frozen meals at a time (UNISON, 2009, p. 2). There is concern that personalisation is actually placing an increased burden on service users and carers. As one told UNISON:

I seem to spend nearly all my time organising care for my severely disabled deafblind son. If a carer is ill, there is no cover ... it takes me hours to organise patchy cover. Therefore it is impossible for me to have any job or life as I have to be around constantly. Bring back properly qualified, trained and vetted homecare – they were wonderful.

(UNISON, 2009, p. 3)

As Ferguson (2007) comments, personalisation can mean that risk and responsibility are shifted from the state to the individual service user or carer, and the implications for rural areas devoid of resource choice and real back-up could be disastrous. Personalisation as a policy extends the commoditisation of social care inherent within the reforms of the early 1990s. Its implementation in England and Wales has resulted in a reduction of publicly provided resources, and a plethora of private profit-making companies that have taken advantage of the new market, often with a diminution of quality of service, and pay and conditions for staff (UNISON, 2009). This reality does not reflect the reinvestment back into communities suggested by Leadbeater and Lownsbrough (2005) with their notions of community capacity building and empowerment. The current climate of public spending reduction, discussed in Chapter 1, can only enhance these contradictions. It remains to be seen whether the financial investment that these authors suggest is required is actually made available or whether personalisation is used to cut services.

Council services in remote and rural areas are important components of the local economy – providing secure employment with reasonable pay and conditions. If social care workers are employed on a permanent contractual basis, they can afford to stay in areas where such employment might not otherwise be readily available. They contribute to local businesses and use local services. A reduction of this type of employment opportunity and the introduction of casualised minimum wage employment, do not offer such security and ultimately may be unattractive to potential employees. This reduces opportunities for service users and contributes to population imbalance and depopulation (already becoming critical as noted in Chapter 1).

Personalisation: realities and resource issues within rural communities

The disability users' movements who lobbied successfully for the introduction of Direct Payments (Barnes, 1997) were drawn in the main from adults with physical disabilities who saw disability as a social issue and were demanding independence and a level playing field. In rural areas, users may accept that geography will mean that physical access and opportunity might be limited out in the community, but they will expect the same support to live independently at home that they might experience in an urban setting. This will include personal care assistance, aids and adaptations and support for carers. Meeting such expectations can be problematic and the Personalisation Agenda will present additional dimensions to such rural and remote service delivery challenges. To explore the issues already outlined in this chapter, some case illustrations will now be presented. These are imaginary but drawn from experience.

Mary is in her late forties and a divorcee living in the small coastal village where she has spent most of her life. Her family had owned a local business, which she had inherited but the effects of multiple sclerosis eventually forced her to sell up several years ago. Mary's grown-up children all live in the city but visit her regularly although none are able to assist with her day-to-day care. The occupational therapist (OT) arranged some basic adaptations that made life easier, such as a downstairs accessible shower, and grant support was provided for this. For a few years Mary managed with one homecare visit on weekdays provided by social services – help being given with essential household hygiene maintenance and shopping. However, confinement to a wheelchair and increasing loss of co-ordination led to worry amongst those who knew her that she was struggling. One morning she was found, by a visitor, on the floor by her bed where she had lain all night having fallen whilst transferring to bed the previous evening. This had happened on previous occasions but she had been able to use a mobile telephone to alert friends who would come round to pick her up and put her back into bed. After this a social worker was asked by her GP to complete a full assessment of her needs and look at services that might enable her to stay at home independently. Mary was central to the assessment and understood when it concluded that to keep safe from harm, she needed care at various times during the day and evening. This included helping her get up, wash and bath, go to bed and toilet. She also needed help with meal preparation, shopping and cleaning her house. She was otherwise regarded as safe on her own and in no need of constant supervision or presence of a carer.

Mary, her social worker and the local care-at-home supervisor discussed together how these agreed services might be delivered. Care-at-home assistants were deployed in the wider community from early in the morning until late in the evening, but as they provided services over a wide rural area, they were unable to meet her choices about when she wanted to get up, go to bed and do other things. It was also recognised that she required support to engage socially in the community and this too was included in her assessed needs. Mary reckoned that she could find people she knew who lived locally who could provide the paid support she needed. Having run a small business with employees in the past, the idea of a direct payment that would enable her to organise her own care appealed, and with the help of a support organisation for users of Direct Payments, she was able to recruit her own small team of carers. These friends and neighbours were easily found because she was well known locally, and in the years since she has been able to retain staff and her situation has been stable. There have been lots of informal spin-offs, and Mary is included in local events and celebrations without recourse to formalised support.

The arrangement was initially a relief to the care-at-home supervisor, whose main problem at that time was how to effectively deploy her scarce staffing resources across a large rural area with constantly fluctuating demand from one small community to another. It also took advantage of the strengths of Mary's situation: her place in her home community and the support she knew she could expect from others to maintain her independence and dignity.

Brian is in his mid-fifties and has a learning disability. Without support he would not eat properly, look after himself or maintain any routines. Until last year many of his needs were met by his ageing mother, but she died and with family support it was agreed he would stay on in the home on his own. Brothers and sisters and their extended families all lived nearby and were willing to help. In recent years Brian had used a daycare service provided through social services several days a week. Through this service his carer had received respite and he had happily socialised and engaged in activities with a small number of other adults with learning disabilities.

After his mother's death, Brian's family asked for a Direct Payment so that they could employ a carer to help Brian with his daily routines. This in turn would help qualify for an Independent Living Fund (ILF) entitlement to increase the hours of a personal assistant (PA). Resource limitations meant that this could only be provided if partially diverted from the daycare resource he had attended. This would reduce his daycare entitlement. The loss of Brian's presence at the daycare resource presented problems for its continuation as another service user had also moved away, leaving only three individuals using a service that employed three part-time workers. The rural setting meant that there was a 'critical mass' issue that threatened the future of the service (Smith and Homer, 2009).

Brian's family duly employed a PA on his behalf. However, their expectations of the individual concerned and their approach to their employment responsibilities resulted in that person only remaining in post for a short period. This pattern has continued and arrangements for his care have only been maintained because the family have been able to plug the gaps themselves. There is concern that if this trend continues the time will soon come where the potential for employment of a PA locally will end.

These two stories represent both possibilities and problems in the rural context. Mary, on the one hand, was able to utilise her place in the community and her natural networks, to mobilise individualised support on an informal and formal level. Funding was provided through the local authority and a service provided beyond that available through normal services. This facilitated empowerment and choice.

Brian, on the other hand, has encountered a different experience. His choice (or that exercised on his behalf by his family, which might in itself be an issue) has resulted in a shift of resources to an individualised service, the result of which is a threat to a local authority-provided respite and daycare service. The loss of this service could potentially result in other users having to also accept an individualised service – or even no service at all, depending on assessment of their needs and where they might fit with eligibility criteria. Those without the capacity to manage their own service might finish up with nothing at all. Brian himself may also miss the company of his friends at the daycare resource and lose out in social terms if not given other opportunities. Whilst the overall promise of personalisation might involve the community capacity building that could invigorate such opportunities for him and other users of the threatened service on an informal, or perhaps volunteer-led, basis this might never happen. The development of alternatives would certainly require strategic planning and investment, and might be quite problematic; there are no guarantees that these would meet the individual needs of users.

Brian's other problem is that he might soon find himself unable to recruit personal assistants (PAs) to meet his needs. If this happens the local authority might have no means to carry out their duty of care if their own service provision no longer exists or is otherwise committed. He and his family could potentially end up with no support and his situation might then break down. He might then have to be admitted to a residential care setting or a supported tenancy a distance away in a more populated community where resources are available to help him live independently. The sequence of events described started out as the individualisation of his support, but has ultimately ended up in his removal from his home community and family support. Had resources been secure, none of this might have happened: his PAs might have avoided conflict with their employer if subject to the conditions of service and pay enjoyed by local authority employees. His daycare service might not have been under threat and he could have continued to enjoy the company of his friends in that setting. In a rural area, secure provision of services will almost certainly require subsidy and support due to the critical mass issues referred to elsewhere in this book.

An example of misplaced faith in the market from another area of social care concerns the impact of older people private residential home closures in the island communities of Mull in 1995 (Scottish Islands Network Newsletter, 1995a) and Cumbrae in 2006 (*Evening Times*, Glasgow). With no other provision, both closures removed all choice and ultimately impacted on the public sector with its duty of care. The only guarantee seems to be that in remote rural communities there should be no absolute reliance on the marketplace and that core services should remain within local authorities and health services.

Shifting the balance of care in remote and rural communities

In Scotland a major policy driver in recent years has been that of *shifting the balance of care*, often simply known by its initials 'SBC'. The policy is mentioned in every contemporary health and local government policy document that discusses social care services. In simple social care terms the main issue is to spend less on residential and nursing home care for frail and dependent older people and more on the community services that will help them maintain independence at home. The broader agenda is currently tied in with the Single Outcome Agreements determining the levels of funding each council receives from the Scottish Government, and the government's 'HEAT' (Health improvement, Efficiency, Access and Treatment) targets for Health Boards. The government's Joint Improvement Team (located within NHS Scotland) now focuses on eight specific improvement areas that it describes as an 'overarching framework':

- Maximise flexible and responsive care at home with support for carers.
- Integrate health and social care for people in need and at risk.
- Reduce avoidable unscheduled attendances and admissions to hospital.
- Improve capacity and flow management for scheduled care.
- Extend the range of services outside acute hospitals provided by non-medical practitioners.
- Improve access to care for remote and rural populations.
- Improve palliative and end-of-life care.
- Improve joint use of resources (revenue and capital).

(NHS Scotland, 2009b)

The improvement area in relation to remote and rural services resulted in the creation of the Rural and Remote Implementation Group in 2008, who have produced reports and recommendations that are likely to influence service developments into the new decade. This contribution, as one might expect from its location within a health agency, is dominated by health rather than social care issues; similar emphasis has been noted with previous such initiatives over many years (Hudson, 2008). However, it is useful from the point of view of developing practice and promoting choice, to examine some of the issues arising from this and other contemporary literature.

The imperative for working together and joining up services wherever possible, although featuring as a major issue in policy in health and social care over the past ten years or so, has always been around in rural and remote areas. As discussed in the section on *isolation* in Chapter 2, workers across agencies will tend to naturally seek ways of joint working and mutual support. The associated theme emerging from the contemporary literature is that services should be based on local geography and population profile rather than on any universal template (Craig and Manthorpe, 2000; Smith and Homer, 2009). My own action research into the development of the Joint Futures Agenda on the Isle of Arran, concluded that local ownership and involvement made a greater impact than top-down initiatives (Turbett, 2002).

Smith and Holmer (2009), in their review of remote and rural developments, emphasise that change management has a particular and potentially problematic dynamic in rural communities. Changes perceived as emanating from the outside in relation to core high-profile services such as hospital or residential care provision, unless representing unarguable improvement, are likely to meet with such widespread resistance that they will become impossible to implement. This has been found to be the case in the Highland Council area where plans to privatise residential care provision and close existing council care homes met such opposition that they were abandoned (Inverness Courier, 2007). In small communities a few influential voices can gain disproportionate power because of the interwoven relationships and networks that operate. This can be because the impact of change has not been properly considered and measured within local contexts: the impact on jobs, local businesses and other unintended consequences beyond the immediate value of changes for service users (Smith and Homer, 2009).

The type and remit of care-at-home service delivery will impact on the SBC Agenda in remote rural communities. Whilst there have been moves across Scotland to develop services that provide personal care, services are regarded generally as lower level (less emphasis on personal care) in rural areas than in urban ones (Hudson, 2008). Issues concern how to recruit, train and retain quality staff when need and demand fluctuate (as discussed earlier in this chapter in relation to personalisation), and how to run services across sparsely populated areas – the 'critical mass' effect (Smith and Homer, 2009). The development of overnight care services to meet both planned and unscheduled need is especially problematic. Borders Council is reported to have achieved this across 70 per cent of its area but considers that to extend to the other 30 per cent would be unacceptable in terms of cost (Smith and Homer, 2009). The answer to some of these issues has been to look increasingly to the voluntary sector. The emphasis on this within the Personalisation Agenda has also been discussed above. Whilst voluntary sector providers in some remote areas have been able, through commissioning, to supply services such as daycare, there is not the same record of success in provision of quality care-at-home services (Smith and Homer, 2009).

Telecare – the use of new technologies to monitor vulnerable individuals and keep them safe – is also highlighted in the Joint Improvement Team output (Smith and Homer, 2009). However, the use of community alarms and more sophisticated monitoring equipment is associated in urban areas with mobile teams who can respond to alerts from a central call centre or monitoring station. As with overnight care services, these are generally ruled out for rural remote areas on cost grounds. Community alarm systems in rural areas are usually operated through requests for assistance being passed to volunteer key holders (family members living nearby or neighbours) who are asked to call out emergency services if required. In the Highland Council area, work is underway to examine whether telecare can be extended through offering training and support to such volunteers (Smith and Homer, 2009). The downside of telecare is of course that the user remains isolated and on their own; being required to communicate with their wall to elicit a response from a call centre many miles away.

From the point of view of service users, a major issue in remote and rural areas is that of stigma. Whilst it might seem socially acceptable to have a home help if you are old and frail, the receipt of a support service for those with a mental health condition implies acceptance of such a label, both by the service user, and perhaps by the wider community. If people avoid such labelling and do not seek help or support, preventative treatment and help are not made available and acute crisis requiring hospital admission becomes more likely, therefore affecting SBC. Philo *et al.* (2003) undertook research in the Highland area looking at geographical issues relating to mental health. First, they found difficulty even finding 'locals' (those with longstanding place-generational ties) who were service users or carers to speak to, and most of their research was based on 'incomers' (those who had migrated from elsewhere within the previous 30 years). They then uncovered a number of factors that reinforced the social exclusion of mental health service users in rural and remote areas:

- an absence of 'positive mental health talk' within communities;
- marginalisation and exclusion through deliberate harassment: violence, name calling and ridicule;
- marginalisation through other discriminatory behaviours: petitions, avoidance, embarrassed silences in public places and other 'everyday' acts of exclusion;
- an absence of privacy and fear of constant surveillance – 'twitching curtains';
- a culture of 'resilience' or stoicism whereby the norm is that silence should be maintained in the face of emotional and psychological difficulty;
- worry about gossip and its consequences.

They found that whilst incomers were less likely to be affected by some cultural and repressive norms, they were likely therefore to be excluded for this perceived failure. Indigenous locals with mental health problems were likely to hide their illness and to self-medicate, perhaps through alcohol abuse. Once professional diagnosis and intervention had occurred the experience of community exclusion was likely to begin. These processes can only be countered through breaking down isolation and bringing users together so that confidence can be built through collective activity and expression. The Highland User Group experience proves that remoteness and distance need not be barriers (Philo et al., 2003).

Social work and criminal justice in rural communities

In Scotland, criminal justice social work became a function of local authorities after the implementation of the Social Work (Scotland) Act 1968. In 1991, 100 per cent funding for services was introduced along with

'National Standards' that drew social workers working in criminal justice away from a welfare emphasis to one of addressing and reducing offending behaviour (Waterhouse and McGhee, 1992; McNeill and Whyte, 2007). Increasingly, such work focused on evidence-based practice with cognitive behavioural approaches typically offered on an individual basis (Smith, D, 2002). This went along with a range of community-based options for courts such as community service schemes, which were run and managed by criminal justice social work services. The requirement for a specialist role for criminal justice social work accelerated the trend for other sections in local authority social work to specialise, leading to the fragmentation that is now almost universal.

In 2008, Scottish local authorities deployed between 0.3 and 1.3 staff per 1,000 population in services for offenders (Scottish Government, 2009i). Staffing figures for several authorities in predominantly rural areas are shown in Table 4.1 (with the Scotland total and Dundee City added for comparative purposes).

**Table 4.1   Local authority social work staff employed
in offender services in 2008**

Authority	Total no. of staff	WTE (whole time equivalent)	WTE per 1,000 population
Eilean Siar	6	6	0.4
Highland	68	55	0.4
Orkney Islands	6	6	0.5
Scottish Borders	37	33	0.5
Shetland Islands	8	7	0.5
Dundee City	121	114	1.3
Scotland	2,022	1,840	0.6

Source: Scottish Government (2009k)

Although these rural authorities all show staffing at the lower end of the scale, the variation is slight and differences across Scotland seem to have no obvious urban/rural significance (however, the figures must be treated with caution as some authorities may have outsourced services to other agencies). The difference is of course that staff located in the rural authorities will be covering vast geographical areas and staff may have to travel great distances. Table 4.2 shows some sample criminal justice social work activities for the same areas. These suggest that in line with staffing, criminal justice social work activity does not necessarily diminish in volume the further one travels along the urban-rural continuum. Variation will of course exist between courts – Shetland has one of the highest rates of probation disposal in Scotland.

Table 4.2 Social work criminal justice dample activities 2008-09

Authority	Social inquiry reports	No. per 1,000 pop.	Probation Orders	No. per 1,000 pop.	Community Service Orders	No. per 1,000 pop.
Eilean Siar	141	78.2	39	21.6	21	11.7
Highland	1,906	123.2	306	19.8	274	17.7
Orkney Islands	107	75.9	27	19.2	16	11.4
Scottish Borders	540	69.2	99	12.7	114	14.6
Shetland Islands	125	81.0	53	34.4	27	17.5
Dundee City	2,713	268.0	319	31.5	206	20.3
Scotland	50,981	138.1	9,072	24.6	6,437	17.4

Source: Scottish Government (2010b)

To what extent does this social work activity reflect the reality of rural crime? The perception is that rural crime is low compared with urban areas. This is borne out by evidence: analysis of the Scottish Crime Survey and Scottish Neighbourhood statistics for 2006 by McVie (2008) suggests that the ratio of reported crime in urban areas is almost three times that in rural areas (the gap is said to be narrowing, but this may reflect a reduction in crime in urban areas rather than increases in rural ones). The closest ratio was in relation to 'personal theft' (1:2.1) and the highest 'violence' (1:4.7). McVie found that in rural areas victims were more likely to know the offender, and in general terms to feel safer in their communities – especially in remote rural areas. However, she also found that victims of crime in remote rural areas were most worried about being victimised again, especially in relation to vehicle theft and vandalism. There has been no recent research into rural crime in recent years but two government-sponsored studies were undertaken in the late 1990s (Anderson, 1998; Smyth, 1999). Both highlight concerns in rural areas about young people, and problems arising from drugs, alcohol and consequent disorder, when there are few resources offering diversionary activity. This was a theme discussed in Chapter 3.

The high visibility of offenders in remote and rural areas perhaps places a different imperative on community-based disposals: the carrying out of Community Service Orders is likely to be a far more public affair than in an urban area, with consequent attraction from a community reparation perspective. This can even help offenders regain respect in communities and perhaps help them into employment. McNeill and Whyte (2007) suggest that criminal justice authorities should be making community engagement a strategic priority in order to build what they describe as 'social capital': 'the social networks and relationships within families and wider communities that can create and support opportunities for change' (2007, p. 177). Public knowledge of some offences such as sexual ones may make it impossible for the offender to remain safely within the community and a move away following charges is likely to occur. A locally based social worker supervising a Probation Order will have a clearer understanding of context, and ability therefore to promote effective community engagement.

The figures regarding staffing levels and disposals, when set alongside the difference in crime rates, indicate that courts are more likely to make community-based disposals in rural Scotland. This does not, however, tally with a 1998 government-sponsored research finding that rural areas had difficulties in accessing and provision of social work criminal justice services 'because of the relatively low demand and the reluctance of offenders to attend services outwith their local environment' (Scottish Office Central Research Unit, 1998). It may be that although the uptake and outcome of services is good, specialisation and associated centralisation of services have not served remote areas well: offenders will be allocated social workers located outwith their local communities who are unable therefore to offer a very flexible or responsive service. The perception may therefore be that the service is not a good one. Figures would also suggest that criminal justice workers are equally busy wherever they are based in Scotland and will have little time to focus on the needs of distant communities. Service delivery from a distance away negates the opportunity for the type of community-based developmental work advocated in Chapter 2, even though there is evidence that remote and rural areas might prove fertile ground for such approaches in the criminal justice context. This activity has been given additional impetus with general policy promotion of 'community safety' initiatives, by definition involving partnership working with other agencies, voluntary organisations and community groups (Smith, D, 2002). I argue here that such developments will require locally rather than centrally based criminal justice social workers, and this will involve additional investment.

The 'bodachs': a historical digression

It is not the purpose of this book to delve into history, but a short account of the boarding out of adults with learning disabilities to the Highlands and Islands of Scotland is included here simply because it seems to be unrecorded elsewhere. Within living memory there was a practice to literally farm out individuals over whom the state held guardianship to work placements on farms. The individuals concerned, single men, who, in the terminology of the day, would have been regarded as 'high grade', were placed on farms to work and live for indefinite periods. The practice of making placements is anecdotally said to have reached a peak in World War Two and seems to have continued up until the 1950s and possibly later, as the last retired 'bodachs' (as they were known) have only died off in recent years. The word 'bodach' sounds Gaelic but is not in any dictionary of the language – presumably it is a Gaelicised derivation of 'boarded-out'. The latter had a wider meaning in rural Scottish communities and included children placed with families from large children's homes such as Quarriers. Many of the individuals concerned were well looked after and took their place within farming families. They were certainly expected to work, and given farm routines, which will have been for most of the week. That must, however, have seemed preferable to life in a large institution although it is doubtful if there was any choice given over the decision to move onto a farm. Some, however, were not well looked after, and lived out in the byre, and whilst fed and clothed, were treated little better than the animals. Often they would pass hands from one farmer to another, the paperwork involved being fairly minimal. I have seen inspection notes held by the Mental Welfare Commission and these evidence fairly minimal standards of quality: 'seems well fed and looked after with clean quarters' being a typical comment. The families with whom the people concerned were placed seem to have received minimal information: I recall finding out through enquiry with the Mental Welfare Commission that an individual who had been placed as a young man in the early 1950s some 40 years previously, had ended up in an institution as a result, at least in part, of sexual offences. This information had never been passed on to the receiving family, presumably because someone had decided this was unnecessary.

I remember Tom whose Arran family hosts had taken him on from another farmer in the early 1960s. Responsibility for him had passed down from father to son over the years but his 'family' were proud of how happy his experience with them had been, and they looked after him until, in old age, his health needs rendered this impossible. Tom's proudest possession was an old photograph taken at the Farmers' Show, showing him resplendent in stockman's white coat, holding by rein a prize-winning bull.

The bodachs were traditionally treated within rural and remote communities as third-class citizens unworthy of rights, who were almost the property of the farmer concerned. They were, however, regarded fondly –

many were renowned as great characters who enjoyed a bit of fun in amongst the hard work that was their lot. At one time all the farms in the cultivated areas of Arran had a boarded-out adult, and some had two. Most worked on the land, taking responsibility for ploughing and harrowing using Clydesdale horses and other tasks. Some were 'house bodachs', doing the washing and ironing and other domestic chores. For farmers whose living was in many cases little more than subsistence, this was win-win – they were paid (five shillings per week in World War Two) for each person placed, and for that, got free labour in an age when there were few concerns about health and safety. There were still half a dozen or so individuals enjoying retirement with their farming family hosts when I started working on Arran in 1988. Assuming that the practice spread across other areas of rural Scotland, there must have been many hundreds of such placements. On Arran the bodachs have all now passed on and their memory will soon fade as generations pass. This short summary of an early variety of care in the community is written in their memory.

Key summary points

■ The Personalisation Agenda in a climate of public spending restraint might lead to a reduction of collective provision in remote rural areas. It might also increase recruitment and retention problems. The best guarantee of continued choice for service users, and presence of provision, is continued public ownership of key resources.

■ Rural and remote social work practice has traditionally involved close partnership working with other agencies. Present policy drivers will be best operationalised if the initiative is given to practitioners at the local level.

- Change in remote and rural areas can be affected by the disproportional influence of key individuals. This should be taken into account when planning for service development and change.

- Visibility, invisibility and stigma are powerful forces for service users in rural areas – particularly those affected by mental illness. User groups can help service users cope with their adverse experiences.

- Criminal justice services are already well used in rural and remote areas although there are relatively low levels of offending. Their role might be enhanced through more local delivery of services alongside a community development perspective within criminal justice services.

Recommended further reading

The cited references on remote and rural working that can be accessed through the Scottish Government Joint Improvement Team website represent current strategic thinking in relation to community care issues, and contain many examples of innovative practice from remote and rural areas. The influential paper by Leadbeater and Lownsbrough should be read alongside critical commentary on personalisation such as that by Ferguson. The paper by Philo et al. on mental health is an important piece of research and one of the few on any area of rural and remote issues in Scotland. There seems to be no literature covering rural criminal justice matters in Scotland but the McNeill and Whyte book provides useful discussion about community engagement and social capital building perspectives, which have resonance in the rural context.

Ferguson, I (2007) 'Increasing user choice or privatising risk: the antinomies of Personalisation' *British Journal of Social Work* 37(3), pp. 387-403.

Hudson, B (2008) *Supporting People in Remote and Rural Areas: A framework for analysis* Edinburgh: NHS Scotland Joint Improvement Team, Remote and Rural Implementation Group, www.jitscotland.org.uk/action-areas/rural-and-remote/publications/

Leadbeater, C and Lownsbrough H (2005) *Personalisation and Participation: The future of social care in Scotland* Edinburgh: Social Work Scotland.

McNeill, F and Whyte, B (2007) *Reducing Reoffending: Social work and community justice in Scotland* Cullompton: Willan.

Philo, C, Parr, H and Burns, N (2003) *Social geographies of rural mental health: Experiencing inclusion and exclusion* Glasgow: University of Glasgow, http://web.ges.gla.ac.uk/Projects/WebSite/Main.htm

Smith, M and Homer, T (2009) *A Review of Service Development and Innovation in the Delivery of Joint Health and Social Care and Support Services in Rural and Remote Areas* Edinburgh: HS Scotland Joint Improvement Team, Remote and Rural Implementation Group, www.jitscotland.org.uk/action-areas/rural-and-remote/publications/

Chapter 5

Social Work with Minorities: The Place of the Scottish Gypsy Travellers

Introduction

Few social workers in Scotland's remote and rural areas will see work with ethnic minorities as a major area of activity. However, much mainstream social work is on behalf of service user groups who inhabit the margins of society; hidden ethnic minorities are marginalised and often overlooked, and social workers may have a role in confronting racism and its divisive effects, and in ensuring that a culturally sensitive approach to issues looks further than dominant rural cultures. This chapter looks particularly at Scottish Gypsy Travellers, at their experience, and at the application of human rights-based approaches when social work interventions are indicated.

Ethnic minorities in rural Scotland

The term 'minority' requires some clarification as it can mean different things in different contexts. Prior to the formation of the Scottish Parliament in 1998, racism was not considered to be an issue in Scotland, but a report commissioned by the Scottish Executive in 2001 found issues for minority communities in accessing services, discrimination and racism in all areas of public life (Netto *et al.*, 2001). At that time the term 'ethnic minority' was certainly considered to concern people of non-white ethnicity but there was a realisation that it should be broadened to include Scottish Gypsy Travellers, asylum seekers and refugees. However, the term remains the subject of debate concerning identity, language and ethnicity (Netto, 2008); it should arguably include the large numbers of migrant workers who have come to Scotland, many as a consequence of the enlargement of the European Union (EU) in 2004, because of differences between them and dominant populations of white Scottish and UK born people. This might, for instance, be experienced as economic exploitation. Thus, the term 'minority' has a political meaning in the sense that it indicates the position in society of 'individuals and groups who may lack effective representation, and political power, and whose needs tend to be neglected or ignored' (Pugh and Cheers, 2010, p. 75).

The 2001 Census tells us that non-European ethnic minorities are a small proportion of Scottish rural society: 1.33 per cent of the population of accessible and remote rural areas, compared with 3.7 per cent in large urban areas. Of these, the largest single ethnic group are people who identify themselves as Pakistani and other South Asian origin, followed by Indian and Chinese (Scottish Executive, 2003). Many of those of Asian origin who live in remote and rural areas will be involved in catering businesses and may be relatively transient; a small Pakistani community, now in decline, has existed in Stornoway on Lewis since the 1930s (*The Sunday Times*, 2006).

Racism is an issue in rural areas despite perceptions at one time that this can only exist when minorities become big enough to be noticed (Pugh, 2000). It is considered that racist incidents are under-reported due to the small and isolated populations involved – fear of reprisal, absence of police response and a feeling that nothing can be done to change the attitudes involved, are all cited as reasons for this (de Lima, 2005). In the past, racism has been reported by English-born incomers to rural Scottish areas (Pugh, 2000; BBC News, 2004). Conversely, many rural workers will have heard English-born migrants state that the absence of a black presence in the community was the principal reason they had moved to their new rural Scottish home. The influx of Eastern European migrants, particularly Polish people, since 2004 has affected rural areas in Scotland, contributing positively to local economies, but creating competition within local job markets that has sometimes left indigenous locals without work. However, their presence has probably helped establish rural communities, like urban ones, as more cosmopolitan than they would have seemed for past generations. Black people, however, due to their small numbers, are still likely to feel very exposed in rural settings (Pugh, 2000).

Rural communities can also provide the opportunity for individual acceptance of ethnic minority people because of the social contacts that arise from everyday life. This can be paradoxical, as the risks of marginalisation and discrimination are increased due to obvious difference, high exposure and profile (Pugh and Cheers, 2010). This might explain why in the UK generally, ethnic minority people are choosing to move into rural areas in small but increasing numbers (Pugh, 2000). This is illustrated by examples from Shetland of local campaigns on behalf of minority community members facing deportation: Sakchai Makao, a 23-year-old born in Thailand but resident in Shetland since he was 10-years-old, faced deportation after an offence committed four years previously after the death of a close relative came to light as the result of a national furore concerning offenders from abroad who had not been sent home. The successful community campaign involved a petition signed by 8,000 people (one in three of the island's population) and the support of over a hundred Members of Parliament (MPs) (*Independent on Sunday*, 2006). This followed campaigns in 2004 in Shetland to save two families, one Burmese and one indigeneous Australian, who faced deportation under UK immigration laws (European Network for Indigenous Australian Rights News, undated). In a separate initiative in 2003 the London-based Conservative Party Kirkhope Commission recommended that a reception centre for asylum seekers should be established on a Scottish island: 'These centres would provide a clean, safe, habitable environment but offer no prospects for economic advancement. There would be a low population density in the surrounding area...' (quoted in Scottish Island Network Newsletter, 2003b). The idea that a Scottish island community should be used for what amounts to political imprisonment was unsurprisingly regarded as quite insulting by actual islanders, and seems to have sunk without trace.

A 2001 Scottish Executive study (Netto et al., 2001) focused, amongst other themes, on social care. Although the research on which conclusions were drawn was based principally on the four main cities of Scotland, the study remarked on the widespread dispersal of ethnic minority communities across every area of the country and the implications this might have for the design and delivery of rural social care services. It found that little was known about the issues and needs of such populations but was concerned that services for older people, carers and disabled people were little used by ethnic minorities (Netto et al., 2001, pp. 58-60). It also found that the needs of ethnic minority children in the 'looked after' and 'accommodated' system were not well met; this is echoed by findings concerning the lack of development of fostering services within Gypsy Traveller communities across the UK (Cemlyn et al., 2009, p. 128).

Gay and lesbian people

Pugh and Cheers (2010) consider that the situation of gay men and lesbian women in rural areas is complex. Whilst they might suffer marginalisation and stress as victims of the type of redneck-style intolerance thought to be typical of rural communities, they might also enjoy acceptance and place and they might have moved there by choice. However, a 2003 Scottish conference on gay and lesbian issues in rural areas reported:

Recently, Margaret realised that none of the LGBT [lesbian, gay, bisexual and transgendered] people she knows, except her, lives in the same place where he or she was raised: they have left villages, small towns, islands. We must fight to make sure that when someone

leaves a community it is out of choice and for their own positive
reasons and not because they are driven out through prejudice.
Indeed, the Equal Opportunities Reporters had already discovered
that those in rural areas suffered significantly more incidence of
discrimination and lack of access to services.

(Beyond Barriers, 2004, p. 8)

This quote suggests that there might be a difference between the experiences of those who freely choose to live somewhere, and those who might want to stay in the place which to them is home. Pugh and Cheers (2010) suggest that in rural areas, even if 'out' and accepted, gay and lesbian people may find themselves behaving with restraint in public places so as not to attract unwanted attention. There will be no subculture for them to feel free to be themselves without such restraint, as there might be in a city. Such issues will be even more exaggerated for transgendered men and women.

Scottish Gypsy Travellers – an ethnic minority?

Scottish Gypsy Travellers are the nation's forgotten and invisible minority who are nonetheless often encountered in rural Scotland. They are forgotten because now we no longer need them to prop up the rural economy with their seasonal migrant labour, it seems as if society would prefer to deny them an existence and has pushed them so far into the margins, that many have given up the unequal struggle and disappeared into mainstream society. They are invisible because most of us would prefer not to see or even understand them as an ethnic minority group with their own history and culture. Discrimination is a daily occurrence for Scottish Gypsy Travellers who try and hold onto their distinct lifestyle and culture and, as we shall see, social workers may be called on to play a role in this. Other ethnic minorities suffer persecution and attack from the Far Right, and many of us are revolted by that. Scottish Gypsy Travellers suffer the same attacks from mainstream politicians who would be insulted if told that their views were racist. In 2008 Labour's Brian Donohoe reacted to the untidiness of visiting Irish Travellers in his Ayrshire constituency by attacking the whole Gypsy Traveller community. In the local press he was reported as stating:

> How can these people be referred to as a community when not one representative has agreed to meet with me? They are complete anarchists ... Travellers are terrorising our area ... I accept that some travellers are peaceful people and don't arrive in an area to trash other people's property, but it seems that most of the travellers in Ayrshire seem to want to do just that.
>
> (Irvine Herald, 2008a)

Donohoe followed this up with a debate in the House of Commons on 30 January 2008. His rather vague aim to address the 'problem' of Travellers was expressed in his opening words:

> When I came to this House I had a romantic view of travelling people; I believed that the Gypsy population was made up of good, God-fearing people who listened to and understood the law, and who carried out their duties within it. Over the time that I have been a Member of Parliament, my opinion has been substantially eroded. Those people have become a threat to the community, and the powers-that-be seem powerless to intervene effectively. As individual MPs, we face a brick wall while the problem escalates by the year.
>
> (House of Commons, 2008)

Donohoe's Labour colleague, Jim Sheridan MP for Paisley and Renfrewshire North, came to his aid in defining the 'problem':

> In my experience, the problem is that when we provide camps for travelling people or Gypsies, they then trash the camps. If there is a

camp they have to live in it, but they want to travel throughout the country. The legislation means that if a camp is provided, they have to go to it. In my experience, they trash the camp so that they can go wherever they want in the community.

(House of Commons, 2008)

Donohoe followed this up several months later with his further thoughts on how to deal with the 'problem':

It seems to me that we have two choices ... The first is a policy of zero-tolerance whereby the moment a travelling community set up camp illegally, they are targeted by all relevant organisations such as police, the education and social work departments, work and pensions, customs and excise and trading standards. Inevitably some or all of these organisations would encounter illegalities or irregularities which would result in legal action. The second option is to set up a new self-policing body.

(Irvine Herald, 2008b)

I have quoted Donohoe's activity in particular because he probably does represent a point of view that has some public appeal. However, if his views were directed at asylum seekers or another ethnic minority group it is likely that they would have resulted in more public revulsion than they actually did at the time. The problem, however, as we shall see below, is not so much how Scottish Gypsy Travellers view society (as these politicians would have us believe), but rather how they are treated by the rest of the community. The official caravan sites that so offend Jim Sheridan MP are declining in numbers and can be characterised by a style of stewardship, complete with barbed wire and closed circuit television (CCTV), which only serves to highlight just how different such sites are from the ones enjoyed by Camping and Caravan Club members (from which this community are generally barred from access). When not on official sites, Scottish Gypsy Travellers who wish to pursue a mobile lifestyle are likely to be moved on from their traditional stopovers – that is, if they are not already deliberately blocked off from access.

Whatever their rights as individuals, how correct is Brian Donohoe MP in describing Scottish Gypsy Travellers as not a 'community'? Certainly, they have a rich oral tradition of storytelling, music and customs, celebrated in the works of Scottish Gypsy Traveller folklorists such as Jess Smith (Smith, J, 2002, 2003, 2005). However, this is not in itself proof of separate ethnic identity. Recently, though, the evidence of ethnic identity has been put to legal proof using the criteria established in the House of Lords *Mandla vs Dowell Lee* case in 1983:

- a long shared history, of which the group is conscious as distinguishing it from other groups, and the memory of which it keeps alive;
- a cultural tradition of its own;
- either a common geographical origin, or descent from a small number of common ancestors;
- a common language, not necessarily peculiar to the group;
- a common religion different from that of neighbouring groups or from the general community;
- being a minority or being oppressed by a dominant group within a larger community. (Clark, 2006, p.3)

In 2007, Ken MacLennan, a social worker from Aberdeenshire, was sacked by his employer, the Gypsy Traveller Education and Information Project (GTEIP), a small organisation ostensibly concerned with Gypsy Traveller welfare based in Aberdeen. MacLennan took this employer to an initial Industrial Tribunal in March 2008 on the basis that the conduct that had brought their displeasure had in fact been undertaken in defence of the rights of an ethnic minority, and his right to do so was protected by race relations legislation. The GTEIP successfully argued at this Hearing that

Scottish Gypsy Travellers were not an ethnic minority at all, but descendants of a mix of Romany gypsies and others dispossessed of land over the centuries who had taken to the road. Academic evidence was marshalled to help them with this case. This outcome set back Scottish Gypsy Traveller rights by years as it had previously been assumed that in the absence of any test case in a Scottish court, this group enjoyed the same rights and legal protections as Romany Gypsy Travellers and Irish Travellers elsewhere in the UK. In 2001, the Scottish Parliament had accepted the report and recommendations of its Equal Opportunities Committee on this matter. The 37 recommendations concerning Gypsy Travellers and public sector policy were defined by the second recommendation that stated: 'All legislation and policies should be framed on the understanding that Gypsy Travellers are an ethnic group, until such time as a court decision is made on recognition as a racial group under the Race Relations Act 1976' (Scottish Executive, 2001, p. 2). Another recommendation advised that capitalisation of the term 'Gypsy Traveller' should be adopted by all public bodies.

The case was reported in the national press (*The Herald*, 2008) and in the view of activists began to make a negative difference to the way individuals were being treated by state organisations. However, MacLennan appealed this aspect of his dismissal. Largely on his own and with no legal representation, but with the help of activists from the Scottish Gypsy Traveller Law Reform Coalition (SGTLRC), and some academics with a close interest in the matter, he led his own case. MacLennan, who had a lot to lose and little to gain personally, won his case. His former employer put up no argument on this occasion. The Employment Judge concerned was impressed with the depth and clarity of the evidence offered, the argument being based on the *Mandla vs Dowell* Lee judgment. Important as this victory was, it was far from the type of higher court ruling that Scottish Gypsy Travellers required, and the campaign of the under-resourced and largely ignored SGTLRC continues.

This case emphasises the importance of the ethnic identity issue to Scottish Gypsy Travellers and the danger in the position of those (otherwise) allies and friends, such as the writer and academic Timothy Neate, who argue the case that Scottish Gypsy Travellers have no separate ethnic identity (Neate, 1996). In Scotland the campaign for full legal recognition has recently won support from the British Association of Social Workers (BASW), the Scottish Trades Union Congress (STUC) (following activity with the public sector union UNISON) and Amnesty International (Turbett, 2009b). In December 2009, Katy Clark MP for North Ayrshire (taking a rather more progressive position than her colleague Brian Donohoe) unsuccessfully moved an amendment to the Equality Bill in the Westminster Parliament, and followed this up with an Early Day Motion (EDM) about Scottish Gypsy Traveller rights in March 2010. It is interesting in the light of public attitudes generally to Gypsy Travellers that the EDM had only gained 21 signatures from other MPs by the time Parliament was suspended for the May 2010 General Election.

Scottish Gypsy Travellers and the experience of prejudice and discrimination

The arguments rehearsed in the *MacLennan vs GTEIP* case, and previously highlighted by the Scottish Parliament's Equal Opportunities Committee, are important for the Scottish Gypsy Traveller community because of their continued individual and shared experience of discrimination.

Marginalisation, harassment and attempts to assimilate Scottish Gypsy Travellers have a long history despite the evidence of their centuries-old contribution to rural life through traditional skills such as tinsmithing. This rather mirrors the experience of their Romany and Sinti cousins throughout Europe, the murder of hundreds of thousands of their number in the Nazi Holocaust being an extreme expression of this in the mid-twentieth century. The folklorist Robert Dawson has contributed to our knowledge of Scottish Gypsy Travellers through his research (Dawson, 2007). In 1895, a committee commissioned by the Secretary of State for Scotland into 'habitual offenders, vagrants, beggars and inebriates' (those without accommodation) reported to parliament after long deliberation and hearing dozens of witnesses. Its remit included consideration of Gypsy Travellers (called throughout 'gipsies' or 'tinkers'), whom they included in the category of 'vagrants and beggars'. It heard no evidence from Gypsy Travellers themselves but instead from a succession of officials, landowners, church ministers, police officers and doctors. It heard pleas to outlaw nomadism for reasons of morality and considered other quite drastic measures to grapple with the perceived threat that some imagined Gypsy Travellers posed to the settled community. Typical of those who gave evidence was a Dr McCallum, who concluded his testimony with the following:

> I am afraid I may appear rather hard-hearted and callous in the few words I have had the honour of addressing to you, but I am firmly convinced that the only effective treatment is eradication. For the children I have only pity. For the grown up members, knowing them as I do, I feel sure that all philanthropic efforts based on sentimentality are useless.

(Dawson, 2007, p. 112)

There were, however, more sympathetic witnesses. Some of whom were concerned that Gypsy Travellers had their own marriage ceremony and that their children must therefore be regarded as illegitimate. This was interestingly ruled out as an argument on the grounds that Scottish law regarding marriage was very liberal and did not require a church blessing.

The report concluded that Gypsy Travellers were, in the main, hardworking, honest, child-centred and monogamous (with their downfall being a tendency to drunkenness) but that the state had a duty to ensure that children were educated, and that Gypsy Traveller children not attending school should be rounded up and forced into a more acceptable way of life. This is indeed what happened in some areas of Scotland: children over the age of 7 were seized from their families and transported to the colonies in virtual slavery, never to see their parents again. This practice continued, with a break during World War One, until the outbreak of war in 1939. No wonder many Scottish Gypsy Travellers to this day have an innate suspicion of social workers (Morran, 2002), stemming back to what Cemlyn (2008, p. 157) has described as 'systematic child abduction' and 'cultural genocide'.

To return to our own times, it seems that relative to other types of social progress, matters have not moved on much for Scottish Gypsy Travellers. In their evidence to the Scottish Parliament Equal Opportunities Committee in June 2005, reviewing progress since the acceptance of the 37 recommendations four years earlier, Scottish Gypsy Travellers described their modern-day experiences:

We carried out a survey of young people and 92 per cent said that they had been picked on and called names because of their identity.

We are not regarded as an ethnic minority. It is okay for the newspapers and media to say what they want about Travellers.

People think that they are not being racist if they call a Gypsy Traveller a tinker... Recently someone said (to me) "Your grandfather was a tinker." The person, who is very nice, was not being cheeky; they thought that the term "tinker" was not pejorative at all.

(Scottish Parliament, 2005a, pp. 2-4)

Morran (2002) reported that housed Gypsy Travellers report that they are still referred to by neighbours as 'tinks' and 'minks' even after many years of tenure.

Within education, Gypsy Traveller children will often try and hide their identities, especially in secondary schools: 'One witness told the committee that a teacher had advised her to tell her daughter "not to let onto the other kids" that she was a Gypsy Traveller' (Scottish Parliament, 2005b, p. 14) Another witness to this same Scottish Parliament Equal Opportunities Committee said: 'One of the stunning things about the evidence of what happens to Gypsy Traveller kids in schools is that every single one of them talks about racial harassment.' (2005b, p. 16). In England, Gypsy Travellers were described by the government Department for Education and Skills in 2003 'as the group most at risk in the education system' because of extreme disadvantage in access, inclusion and achievement (quoted in Cemlyn, 2008, p. 159). The situation can hardly be better in Scotland. Government support for the development of education of Scottish Gypsy Traveller children is directed to the Scottish Traveller Education Programme (STEP), a body whose purpose is promotional and advisory rather than targeted on services. It is down to local authorities to make specific provision, the expectation being that they should follow government policy by way of their individual Single Outcome Agreements (see Chapter 1). This should include the 11 recommendations (of the 37 referred to above) on education for Scottish Gypsy Traveller children that the Scottish Parliament recommended in 2001. The implementation of any of these recommendations will be affected by priorities in a climate of financial restraint, and also by general public attitudes towards Scottish Gypsy Travellers.

Gypsy Travellers continue to be the target of racial abuse, sometimes promoted and encouraged by the tabloid press. In 2005, under the headline 'STAMP ON THE CAMPS', *The Sun* newspaper made a call to its readers:

The Sun today launches a campaign to STOP John Prescott giving the green light to illegal gipsy [sic] camps across Britain.

The Deputy Prime Minister has ordered local councils to go soft on travellers' camps and turn a blind eye to the shocking problems they create.

But The Sun, on behalf of our ten million readers, is determined to fight him all the way.

(*The Sun*, 2005)

This article prompted concern that it would encourage physical attacks on Gypsy Travellers (BBC News, 2005). *The Sun*, however, was following a long tradition in the local and national press typified by the following from the front cover of the *Birmingham Evening Mail* of 29 June 1993:

KEEP THIS SCUM OUT (And it is time to hound 'em Chief Constable). They call themselves tinkers, itinerants, new age travellers. We call them parasites. The scum of the earth who live off the backs of others. They contribute nothing but trouble ... They set up filthy disease-ridden camps on roadsides and in parks and offend every decent citizen.

(quoted in Morris, 2000, p. 214)

In Scotland, the *Aberdeen Evening Express* has been particularly criticised for its reporting of Gypsy Traveller issues and was taken by the Commission for Racial Equality (CRE) to the Press Complaints Commission in 2005, along with several other regional newspapers (CRE, 2005). However, the usefulness of making such complaints has been questioned in the past: between 1991 and 2000, over 600 complaints about racism in the press were raised, none of which was upheld because of their particular rules (Morris, 2000).

Between 2000 and 2007, the proportion of Scottish Gypsy Traveller survey respondents who reported being the subject of prejudice or harassment in the preceding twelve-month period rose from 62 per cent to 79 per cent (Taggart, 2008). This is borne out by the latest Scottish Social Attitudes Survey (conducted in 2006): 25 per cent of respondents (the largest response concerning any minority group) thought that a Gypsy Traveller would be 'very unsuitable' as a primary school teacher; 32 per cent of respondents would be 'happy' or 'very happy' if a close relative married or formed a long-term relationship with a Gypsy Traveller (two thirds would therefore not be). The authors concluded: 'Evidently discriminatory attitudes towards Gypsies/Travellers are widely held in Scottish society' (Bromley *et al.*, 2007, p. 31). A recent report from the Equality and Human Rights Commission (EHRC) quotes a Scottish activist who responded to its UK-wide consultation: 'it is socially acceptable to be racist towards Gypsies and Travellers – numerous examples in media, policies and practices of public bodies' (Cemlyn et al., 2009, p. 210). One of the witnesses to the Scottish Parliament Equal Opportunities Committee told of how 'I had some friends up north, and there was a bit on the news about them. Some of the teenagers from the village came down and stoned them. They broke the windows of my friend's car and caravan' (Scottish Parliament, 2005a, p. 14).

Clearly, press attack (which may include the remarks of MPs and other community leaders) carries the danger of fuelling racist violence at local level.

Health has long been a concern and six of the Scottish Government's 37 recommendations in 2001 concerned ways to address health inequalities (Scottish Executive, 2001). Gypsy Travellers who took part in a UK-wide study were found to have significantly poorer health than the lowest socio-economic group population, with previous research showing higher childhood accidents, a higher proportion of babies of low birthweight, and higher death rates from cardio-vascular disease (Van Cleemput and Parry, 2001). Infant mortality in Gypsy Travellers in the UK has been reported as three times that of the general population, and overall life expectancy lower than for the general population – twelve years for women and ten years for men (Cemlyn et al., 2009). Despite this poorer health, Gypsy Travellers use health services less than others in the population (Cemlyn et al., 2009). Access to health provision was reported to the Scottish Parliament Equal Opportunities Committee in 2005 as an ongoing issue: Save the Children, a voluntary sector organisation working with young Scottish Gypsy Travellers, advised:

How will a 14-year old young woman who lives in a roadside camp on the outskirts of a town and whose reading and writing is not brilliant get access to information about her health needs?

(Scottish Parliament, 2005b, p. 13)

Another witness told the Committee:

> ... if someone tries to register with a general practitioner, they are told, "We don't do caravan people." The next time they try and register they are told, "Oh, there's a waiting list."

(Scottish Parliament, 2005a, p. 2)

The now disbanded UK National Association of Health Workers with Travellers (NAHWT) told EHRC researchers in 2009: 'the most common problem for Travellers is difficulty in accessing primary care through GPs because of their insistence in having a permanent address' (Cemlyn et al., 2009, p. 52). If registration is only given on a temporary basis, there is exclusion from various services including screening; a reliance on walk-in and Accident & Emergency facilities means that there is no follow-up or continuity of care (Cemlyn et al., 2009). In Scotland there is no dedicated and funded advocacy resource for Gypsy Travellers over such issues; on an informal basis, members of the SGTLRC attempt to provide such a service and a number of sympathetic non-Traveller professionals are involved in giving informal advice to Gypsy Traveller activists. The National Resource Centre for Ethnic Minority Health undertook some research to look at access to health needs assessments by Scottish Gypsy Travellers in the North of Scotland in 2006. Their recommendations suggested the importance of:

- developing health needs assessments around events planned with the Gypsy Traveller community;
- acknowledging and planning for diversity within the Gypsy Traveller community;
- documenting and recording all data.

(National Resource Centre for Ethnic Minority Health, 2006)

Public efforts to intervene in the provision of accommodation for Scottish

Gypsy Travellers go back to the post-war years. In 1945, Perthshire County Council set up the Bobbin Mill site on privately donated land in Pitlochry, Perthshire. This was officially established as a 'tinker experiment' to encourage Gypsy Travellers to abandon their lifestyle and move 'upwards' into settled council housing (Taylor, 2004). The language used in letters and correspondence surrounding the establishment of Bobbin Mill reflects a condescending and patronising form of racism that may have been standard at the time, but which unacceptably continues to this day (these archives are held in Perth Library). The huts provided were of a deliberately low standard to promote the process of assimilation into mainstream living. The experiment failed as the tenants settled into their accommodation and most showed no interest in giving up their way of life and culture. Sixty-five years later, the site is still occupied and only now, after many years of campaigning, is being upgraded by the council to include such basic amenities as electricity and running water.

The 2009 research report into Gypsy Traveller issues commissioned by the EHRC considered that the question of accommodation was 'the key to understanding the inequalities and barriers to service access experienced by Gypsies and Travellers' (Cemlyn et al., 2009, p. 5). Within twenty-first century UK society, settled accommodation brings the benefits of eligibility and access to health, education and other public services. The report considered that without decent accommodation, Gypsies and Travellers risk being pushed 'further and further into poverty, social exclusion and "cultural shock"' (Cemlyn et al., 2009, p. 5). Those who particularly choose to maintain (there may indeed be little choice) a mobile lifestyle may find themselves not accepted as communities and official agencies seeking to move them on so they are someone else's responsibility.

In 1971, the Scottish Office introduced a system of grant funding to enable local councils to establish sites for Gypsy Travellers in their areas. This took many years to get under way but by 2002, 39 sites had been established in 27 local authority areas, including three for seasonal use only. The three island areas determined that they had no requirement for provision, and more controversially, three authorities (East Ayrshire, East Renfrewshire and Inverclyde) made no provision at all (Scottish Executive Social Research, 2005). By 2009, the number of year-round provided sites had reduced to 32, and actual pitches (individual places for households) had reduced from 562 to 499 (Scottish Government Social Research, 2009). The sites that had closed were said to have done so because of disuse or vandalism. A further site (Glasgow) has since closed permanently. Actual household numbers on provided sites remained much the same between 2005 and 2009, but the number of individuals had increased from 1,370 to 1,590 (Scottish Government Social Research, 2009). As 45 per cent of these occupants were under the age of 19, one wonders where these young people might have gone once they had outgrown their parental homes. One answer seems to lie in the increased number of unauthorised sites under occupation in the winter count – between 2001 and 2009 the proportion of caravan-dwelling Scottish Gypsy Travellers on 'unauthorised sites' rose from 11 per cent to 22 per cent (Scottish Government Social Research, 2009). Gypsy Travellers who occupy such sites rely totally on local official and unofficial tolerance (the former might depend on the latter) as they enjoy no legal protection. Indeed, the 1994 Criminal Justice and Public Order Act made it illegal for Gypsy Travellers to stop other than on authorised publicly provided or private caravan sites. The latter will often turn away Gypsy Travellers. However, increasingly in the UK, Gypsy Travellers are buying or renting land and setting up their own sites (Cemlyn et al., 2009). Traditional sites are increasingly blocked off and barred from access.

One of the factors consistently overlooked and ignored by official agencies is the Scottish Gypsy Traveller clan or family tradition of living closely to one another. The establishment of an official site has in the past been used as an excuse to force Travellers from their traditional stopping places, which often had family associations, and into situations of potential conflict with other families. It is for this reason that some sites just have not worked, rather than because of any tendency towards alleged anti-social behaviour.

In 2006, ten local authority sites were considered to have environmental nuisance issues such as proximity to pylons (four sites), proximity to motorways (four sites), flood risk (three sites), proximity to electricity sub-stations (two sites) and proximity to landfill sites (two sites) – lending credence to Gypsy Traveller beliefs that many publicly provided sites were on land that no-one else wanted and that would certainly not be acceptable for mainstream housing by the settled community (Communities Scotland, 2006). Again, it might be no surprise if some Gypsy Travellers who find themselves on such sites because of the lack of any alternative, reciprocate the lack of respect shown to their culture and way of life by the settled community.

Another Scottish Executive (2001) recommendation concerned the establishment by local authorities of Gypsy Traveller liaison officer posts. This was considered important if needs and requirements were to be properly identified in collaboration with Gypsy Travellers themselves; again, this recommendation was left by government to councils to decide for themselves whether to implement and in what form. By 2006, twelve councils had simply added this task to the remits of their existing site wardens (Communities Scotland, 2006), a move criticised as tokenistic by Gypsy Traveller representatives (Scottish Parliament, 2005b). Only four had appointed dedicated Gypsy Traveller liaison officers (Communities Scotland, 2006). The evidence would suggest that little progress has been made in tackling discrimination and providing equal opportunities for Scottish Gypsy Travellers. This despite the 2001 recommendations of the Scottish Parliament. By 2006, eight Scottish local authorities still did not even recognise Scottish Gypsy Travellers as an ethnic minority (Communities Scotland, 2006).

Social work and Scottish Gypsy Travellers

As has been noted already, Scottish Gypsy Travellers, who are a small community with a long memory of marginalisation and oppression, have good reason to be mistrustful of social workers and other state officials who might want to intervene in their lives from a perspective of what wider society might support as welfare concern. The assessment criteria used by health and welfare professionals are likely to be those used for settled communities, and will often involve judgements about compliance or otherwise with formal and informal codes of conduct (Cemlyn, 2008). This also applies to those Scottish Gypsy Travellers who have settled into housing, but who, as we have seen, continue to suffer from prejudice and racist abuse, but who are even less recognised as a minority (Morran, 2002). This will now be examined through a case study drawn from a real-life situation known to the SGTLRC.

The **G** family were made up of Mr and Mrs G (they were not formally married but had been together since their teens) and their three children: two sons aged 18 and 14, and a daughter aged 10. The family had lived in settled housing for short periods but had reverted to a caravan-based travelling lifestyle in central Scotland. Mr G had a pick-up truck and bought and sold scrap metal, a traditional Gypsy Traveller occupation. They came to the attention of the authorities when they moved their caravan onto a piece of land on the fringes of a small town. This was with the permission of the landowner, a rent being agreed. Complaints from neighbours about the presence of the caravan were initially dealt with by planning officers of the local council, as there was no formal planning permission. The school-age children were not attending school although it was known that they had done so elsewhere, the parents complaining of hostility towards them in both the primary school that the youngest child attended, and the secondary school attended by the youngest son. The youngest son was subsequently reported by neighbours as being out with his father and brother collecting scrap metal during school hours. The parents were bewildered by the attitudes they encountered from the local authority who clearly told them to move to another area (the provided site some distance away was full). They became hostile in general terms although they did agree to discuss their children's education with officials, with the result that some home-based education was arranged for both children. Meantime, neighbour complaints and police involvement resulted in a referral to the council's Anti-Social Behaviour Team (known as the ASBO team), who involved the local children and family social work team because of perceptions that the children's needs were being neglected. The family's reaction to all this attention became increasingly more hostile, including to the social workers who tried to assess the children's situation. This led on to a child protection case conference that the parents had little understanding of, and the placement of the two children on the child protection register as at risk of neglect. The home school teacher actually started after this and soon found that initial perceptions were misguided. However, the situation was moving on apace with intention served on the family to eject them from the site where they lived without making any other alternative available. Neither parent was particularly literate so there was little understanding of official letters and notices.

At this point, the SGTLRC was contacted (not an easy task as it has no office or staff) and arranged to provide an advocate for the family at the child protection review case conference. The advocate attended the case conference and succeeded in persuading the multi-agency group present of their duty to adopt a more considered and culturally relative approach. She was able to articulately explain the situation from the family's perspective within the context of Scottish Gypsy Traveller culture. The advocate questioned the basis of the child protection concerns as there was no evidence of risk of significant harm, but it was clear that the family required support, including for the children. The children's names were removed from the child protection register and a multi-agency plan devised to support the family and help them settle where they were.

This case illustrates a number of issues that can arise at the interface between isolated Gypsy Travellers and authority. First, the reaction of neighbours to the presence of the family was an unfortunate one arising from the prejudice that, as we have seen in this chapter, is only too commonly found. Unless council officials have received awareness training that can help them identify prejudice, they can easily find themselves acting from a fundamentally flawed and questionable basis. The presence of a Gypsy Traveller liaison officer who has connections with the Gypsy Traveller community (who will ideally have been involved in their appointment) can help avoid such issues. Second, Gypsy Travellers often lack formal education and can be easily pushed into a defensive position that is interpreted as a threat by others; again, a culturally sensitive approach might avoid this. Third, the use of ASBO legislation is reported as being common in dealing with perceived problems with Gypsy Travellers (Cemlyn, 2008). ASBOs rely on assumptions about what behaviour a community believes is right for itself, as its success depends on the reporting of behaviour and its ongoing measurement against standards framed in the ASBO. Their use to police a community within (or in this case outside) a community must be challenged as inappropriate from any ethical standpoint. Finally, it can be seen even from the brief detail provided that eventually a sensitive assessment of the children within the context of their family and culture resulted in engagement and positive outcomes for all concerned.

This case example illustrates a situation in which an understanding and appreciation of Gypsy Traveller culture and lifestyle might have helped avoid discriminatory practice. Practice was both discriminatory and oppressive even though the workers concerned were unlikely to have perceived this for themselves. Cemlyn (2008, p. 161) argues that a human rights approach can help social workers to approach work with Gypsy Travellers in a culturally sensitive manner: 'the failure to recognise ethnic status leads to inattention to cultural and race equality issues'. This might have been written for the G family, as might Cemlyn's rejoinder that:

Engagement ... with Travellers' cultural perspectives and daily experiences would identify the risks from having nowhere safe to live, no basic facilities and facing the trauma of eviction. Required services could be reframed as basic rights to water, sanitation and safety...

narrow categories of risk and protection would be challenged by a structurally and culturally informed analysis.

(Cemlyn, 2008, p. 166)

However, Cemlyn suggests that social work is increasingly moving in the opposite direction and quotes research showing that graduating English social work students 'preferred micro goals and practice within a statutory framework, giving less attention to macro goals' (2008, p. 163). Ife (2008, p. 184) argues that social work undertaken from a human rights perspective must incorporate both micro and macro goals and avoid falling into one or other perspective – always seeing 'the personal and the political'. This, as has been argued elsewhere in this book, is crucial to rural-based social work where the context of practice is all important.

A human rights approach rests on legal authority arising from United Nations, European and the corresponding UK legislation: the 1998 Human Rights Act. The European Convention on Human Rights (ECHR) has been strengthened through case law: Article 8 now includes 'the right to respect for the traditional way of life of a minority' (quoted in Cemlyn, 2008, p. 160). The UK legislation has been applied with success to prevent UK Travellers being evicted from unauthorised sites in England and Wales. Court hearings must now weigh factors such as hardship, the impact on health and education and the availability of alternative sites (2008). Social workers in Scotland are obliged to fulfill the Code of Practice that states: 'As a social service worker you must protect the rights and promote the interests of service users and carers', specifically including 'respecting diversity and different cultures and values' (Scottish Social Services Council, 2009, section one). The International Federation of Social Workers (IFSW) takes this a step further. Its statement of principles concerning ethics includes the following:

4.2. Social Justice

Social workers have a responsibility to promote social justice, in relation to society generally, and in relation to the people with whom they work. This means:

1. Challenging negative discrimination* –Social workers have a responsibility to challenge negative discrimination on the basis of characteristics such as ability, age, culture, gender or sex, marital status, socio-economic status, political opinions, skin colour, racial or other physical characteristics, sexual orientation, or spiritual beliefs.

*In some countries the term "discrimination" would be used instead of "negative discrimination". The word negative is used here because in some countries the term "positive discrimination" is also used. Positive discrimination is also known as "affirmative action". Positive discrimination or affirmative action means positive steps taken to redress the effects of historical discrimination against the groups named in clause 4.2.1 above.

2. Recognising diversity – Social workers should recognise and respect the ethnic and cultural diversity of the societies in which they practise, taking account of individual, family, group and community differences.

3. Distributing resources equitably – Social workers should ensure that resources at their disposal are distributed fairly, according to need.

4. Challenging unjust policies and practices – Social workers have a duty to bring to the attention of their employers, policy makers, politicians and the general public situations where resources are inadequate or where distribution of resources, policies and practices are oppressive, unfair or harmful.

5. *Working in solidarity – Social workers have an obligation to challenge social conditions that contribute to social exclusion, stigmatization or subjugation, and to work towards an inclusive society.* (IFSW, 2004, unpaginated)

Many Scottish Gypsy Travellers will not know their rights and may not offer any effective challenge to the oppressive practices of external authority. Social workers, with their implicit value base and Codes of Practice, must ensure that practice in relation to this group has a human rights, culturally sensitive base, and not one arising from local (and national) mainstream culture and perception. This should be used to promote inclusion, social justice and anti-discrimination. Our actions in using the Scottish Social Services Council (SSSC) Codes of Practice as a basis for such activity helps convert the IFSW codes from an aspirational document to a real guide for good practice.

The 2009 EHRC report contains a number of important recommendations concerning social work services across the UK, including the following:

- Gypsies and Travellers need to be welcomed into policy forums in order to assist in tackling some of the dilemmas inherent in social work with the communities.
- Recognition of ethnic minority and cultural status and inclusion in racial equality strategies and training are essential.
- The situation of Gypsy and Traveller children in contact with social work services should be assessed holistically, making full use of all dimensions of the 'Assessment Triangle', including structural, discriminatory and cultural factors.
- Culturally appropriate services, for example, in relation to fostering and carer support, need to be developed in consultation with communities.
- The safeguarding of children from short-term and long-term harm during evictions should be the responsibility of local Safeguarding

Children Boards. *(Author's note: in Scotland this might fall within the remit of local Child Protection Committees.)*

- Research was required in a number of areas including: the impact on Gypsy and Traveller children of evictions; on the experience generally of children with social work services; on provision for disabled Gypsy and Traveller children; on the experience of older and disabled Gypsy and Traveller people and their carers with social work services.

- Contradictory government policies that promote inclusion while also requiring monitoring, surveillance and exclusion should be further analysed. The humanitarian and egalitarian basis of social work should be more clearly articulated at practice and policy levels in this process.

- Social work should add its voice much more clearly at organisational and leadership levels to calls for basic accommodation and other rights for Gypsies and Travellers.

- Anti-racist training for social work staff needs to recognise Gypsies' and Travellers' minority ethnic and cultural status and requirements, with involvement from members of the communities.

- Social work services should be aware of, and distance themselves from, the oppression associated with enforcement actions relating to accommodation, and from more hidden forms of control involved in surveillance.

- A human rights approach needs to be further developed in social work theory and practice alongside existing approaches that promote equality practice. (Cemlyn *et al.*, 2009)

These recommendations need to be pursued by local authorities and addressed by individual workers in their everyday practice.

General conclusion

Clearly, social workers have a duty to challenge racism and homophobism, whatever form it takes, and the advice about challenges to accepted orthodoxy given in Chapters 2 and 3 apply here too. A social work practice that recognises and appreciates the dynamic of social difference (including race) as an essential component of anti-oppressive practice (Burke and Harrison, 2002) should be just as much a part of the rural agenda as an urban one. It has been suggested that social workers need to commence this process by examining their own attitudes and those they find in the setting they work in (Thompson, 2001), rather in the way that this was suggested in Chapter 3 in respect of patriarchy. Cultural relativism, suggested as an important component of rural practice in Chapter 2, must be based on the needs and cultures of minority groups and not merely compliant with dominant rural belief systems.

Key summary points

■ Scotland's minorities, including ethnic minorities, make up a very small proportion of the rural population. The high profile of ethnic minorities in rural areas can result in racist attack and this is often under-reported.

■ Gypsy Travellers are a long standing but especially marginalised group, whose status as an ethnic minority remains precarious despite a recent legal ruling in their favour.

■ Social workers who encounter Scottish Gypsy Travellers have a duty to ensure that a culturally sensitive approach to assessment of need includes the context of the individual and/or family within their own community, and not just their geographical one. Support for such human rights-based practice can be found within ethical frameworks and the SSSC Codes of Practice.

Recommended further reading

The de Lima paper and the report by Beyond Barriers both give useful insights into the issues facing ethnic minorities and the LGBT community respectively in rural Scotland. The 2009 EHRC report, authored by Cemlyn et al., provides a great deal of useful background information on the discrimination faced by UK Travellers, including Scottish Gypsy Travellers, and is downloadable from the internet. The BJSW paper by Cemlyn is especially useful in guiding social work interventions. Clark's paper, available online, provides a detailed justification for legal minority ethnicity for Scottish Gypsy Travellers.

Beyond Barriers (2004) *Linking Scotland, Planning Futures: Report of Beyond Barriers National Conference on the needs of LGBT people in rural and remote Scotland* Glasgow: Beyond Barriers.

Cemlyn, S (2008) 'Human rights and Gypsy Travellers : An exploration of the application of a human rights perspective to social work with a minority community in Britain.' *British Journal of Social Work* **38(1),** pp. 153-73.

Cemlyn, S, Greenfields, M Burnett, S, Matthews, Z and Whitwell, C (2009) *Inequalities Experienced by Gypsy and Traveller Communities: A review* Manchester: Equality and Human Rights Commission, www.equalityhumanrights.com/uploaded_files/research/12inequalities_experienced_by_gypsy_and_traveller_co mmunities_a_review.pdf

Clark, C 'Defining ethnicity in a cultural and socio-legal context: the case of Scottish Gypsy-Travellers' *Scottish Affairs* **54** Winter 2006 pp. 39-67, www.scottishaffairs.org/onlinepub/sa/clark_sa54_winter06.html

de Lima, P (2005) *Addressing Racial Harrassment in Rural Communities*, www.cjscotland.org.uk/index.php/cjscotland/dynamic_page/?title=racial_harrassment

Chapter 6

The Management and Organisation of Rural Services and the Use of Communication Technologies

Introduction

This chapter looks at the organisation of rural services, including the means by which they might be managed: in keeping with the agendas of employing organisations but at the same time meeting the real needs of service users and staff. It also looks at the use of new technology in various aspects of organisation and practice in rural settings.

Organisational form

The 32 local authorities in Scotland have all developed their own organisational structures that vary according to geography and population size, and in theory at least, are reflective of local circumstance and priority determination. Services they provide are all as agreed with the Scottish Government according to individual Single Outcome Agreements (SOAs) between government and local authorities. SOAs reflect the fifteen national outcomes that describe what the Scottish Government wishes to achieve over the ten-year period from 2007; for example: 'we live longer, healthier lives' and 'we have tackled the significant inequalities in Scottish society' (Scottish Government, 2010c). An overview of inspections of all local authority social services in Scotland offered no template for social services organisation despite criticism in various individual inspection reports over leadership and organisational matters (SWIA, 2010). The inspection methodology was in fact based on a universal 'performance inspection model' and geographical issues concerning service design and delivery were not addressed in the individual inspection reports (Turbett, 2009a).

This lack of central direction or guidance seems unfortunate. In Chapter 2 reference was made to the call in *Changing Lives* (Scottish Executive, 2006) to ensure that models fit the reality of social work in remote areas. It is to be hoped that organisational change affecting rural and remote areas is not based on urban models of service delivery and quality assurance. The most important element of this is to ensure that flexibility is maintained and unhelpful fragmentation avoided. Given the unique pressures on rurally based workers, described in Chapter 2, it does not seem productive to manage remotely based social workers through separate teams even if their roles are specialised. The answers to the issues this raises will vary from location to location and between authorities, but the underlying principle is that sound rural solutions should be sought for rural problems.

One important organisational issue is whether to provide services from centralised bases or distributed services that are spread over wide areas by staff who might therefore work in isolation from one another (Pugh and Cheers, 2010). The former will involve considerable staff time lost in travel but may group staff effectively for peer support, supervision and the avoidance of other problematic issues that are discussed in this chapter. This is sometimes described as 'hub and spoke' or 'satellite' service provision. Some Scottish authorities operate a mix: on the Isle of Mull, community care and reception services are operated by locally based staff, whilst children and family services are delivered from the mainland – a 45-minute ferry journey away. Pugh and Cheers (2010, p. 127) report research that shows that 'occasional satellite services are most effective when linked with an existing, ongoing front line service that can provide support and can act as the initial point of contact'. Decisions will be based on demand, travel options as well as budgetary constraints. However, in Australia, for example, considerable tension is reported by managers of outreach staff over access to vehicles (staff are often flying into localities) and administrative and reception issues (Lehmann, 2005).

In Scotland, a recent organisational development has been the introduction into some areas of community health and social care partnerships (CHSCPs – sometimes under similar but different titles) to bring together local authority social services and health run agencies under common management. This follows the previous Joint Futures policy (Scottish Executive, 2000) that had similar if less specific aims. CHSCPs have been pioneered in Glasgow but their introduction in Orkney suggests applicability in the rural and remote setting. However, as suggested in Chapter 2, close inter-agency co-operation and working has always been a feature of remote rural practice and whether investment in new management structures will enhance this process remains to be seen. These initiatives have been given a recent boost by the findings of the Arbuthnott (2009) review of local authority services in the Clyde Valley (Glasgow City and neighbouring authorities), a paper designed to address the financial pressures and 'more-for-less' agenda referred to in Chapter 1.

Management and supervision of staff

Issues relating to the importance of good supervision and workload management are now generally acknowledged (Coulshed and Mullender, 2006). Rural literature in the past tended to emphasise the requirement for workers to be self-sufficient in their isolation (e.g. Ginsberg, 1998b, p. 18) but this should no longer be considered acceptable. In the rural context the debate has shifted from whether supervision *should* be made available, to how it *can* be made available (Pugh and Cheers, 2010). The general organisational need for more control over staff reflects the rise of managerialism (see below) in social work, but this is a lesser issue from a frontline perspective. Supervision need not be about managerial control, but has other supportive functions: administrative, educational and the sharing of decision making (Coulshed and Mullender, 2006). The reality for social workers and their frontline managers generally, as we shall see below, is one of reduced autonomy, exposure to risk and therefore an increased requirement for validation and support from managers and employing organisations. *Changing Lives* seems rather out of step with other contemporary literature, with its emphasis on 'professional autonomy within a framework of accountability' (Scottish Executive, 2006, p. 51) (a notion that indeed seems rather contradictory) and lack of reference to supervision.

Managerialism is associated with the 'new public management' that rolled out from the early 1990s across the public sector. The principal emphasis of this trend has been 'contracting out service delivery from the public sector to the private and voluntary sectors and applying ideas drawn from business management that focus on securing more economic, efficient and effective services' (Harris, 2007, p. 20). Within this framework, managers are given power and authority over professionals to bring about change and work towards prescribed targets and performance indicators, with an emphasis on cost cutting and efficiencies (Harris, 2007). Social services organisations were particularly vulnerable to new public management managerial styles. One of the most respected commentators on social work in the UK, Olive Stevenson (2005), in a paper reviewing the past 40 years, writes that the development of the profession should be seen in the context of four key factors: organisational turbulence; the years of Conservative Government from 1979 to 1997; the era of child protection inquiries; and the rise of managerialism. All are of course linked: a profession under attack for perceived incompetence in a climate of public spending cuts and political attacks on the welfare state. The response to the anxiety that this all provoked, Stevenson contends, was a tightening of control through improved management systems and structures, and managerialist approaches fitted the bill. Along with them came inspection regimes, an emphasis on complaints procedures and regarding service users as customers or consumers who can make choices within markets, and a role for managers as gatekeepers. Managerialism is viewed as a de-professionalising process and has been criticised by some commentators as being to blame for low morale and dissonance between professional training and actual practice (Stevenson, 2005; Ferguson and Woodward, 2009).

All this will be recognisable to anyone working in a contemporary Scottish social services setting. The system requires managers and structures that appear to support these aims, and they will be found in one form or another in even the most remote setting. However, managerialism has perhaps had a lesser impact on remote and rural social work organisation because some of the elements have been missing: the personal nature of relationships and the absence of markets (as described in Chapters 2 and 3) may have prevented some incursions.

Discussion of rural and remotely based services necessarily focuses on frontline activity and having discussed briefly how this might be impacted by top-down managerialist agendas, we now need to look at how the needs of rural and remotely based staff can best be met and what the particular pressures might be for frontline supervisors.

Workload management seems poorly understood as a concept, often assumed as being in place when the evidence suggests that it is not. A recent Social Work Inspection Agency (SWIA) review of inspections of all Scotland's 32 authorities states that only a few had any type of workload management scheme in place (SWIA, 2010). At the same time, social workers often complain of excessive workloads (Jones, 2001). This is the subject of a major campaign by the main trade union representing social workers in Scotland, UNISON, and the professional association BASW, with the publication of a straightforward negotiating guide to workload management and supervision (UNISON Scotland and BASW, 2010). Absence of effective workload management exposes frontline staff to unrealistic expectation about work output (self-imposed as well as external), consequent dangerous practice, stress, burnout and other health problems.

Pugh and Cheers (2010) suggest that the presence of supervision and workload management positively impacts on retention of staff in rural settings. They also state that this and job satisfaction are also influenced by adequate administrative provision, minimisation of after hours work and travel, career development opportunities, worker autonomy and minimised workplace conflict. These are all onerous responsibilities if frontline managers are equally isolated, and recognition by agencies of such issues should guide training, resourcing and support of supervisory staff.

The isolation experienced by remotely based social workers is no excuse for poor attention to workload management and supervision issues, but this does present recognised challenges to employers (SWIA, 2010). Indeed, the serious implications of such isolation, and the pressures concerning dual relationships and confidentiality (discussed in more detail in Chapter 2) suggest that this is of absolute importance. These issues bring their own pressures upon supervisors, particularly within the managerialist climate of contemporary practice. The drive to rationalise and achieve efficiencies within a competitive market framework is very problematic in a rural locality when there are issues of critical mass (as discussed in Chapter 4 in relation to the Personalisation Agenda). Such tensions may be poorly understood by senior managers in agencies who are based elsewhere. They may also be misunderstood for different reasons by community partners and collaborators. Roles can overlap, and loyalties might be tested: are local managers with their local communities, or with their large outside employing organisations whose motives are possibly mistrusted? This is a factor commented on in Chapter 4 in relation to management of change in remote rural areas.

As community members themselves, who willingly take on other leadership roles because of their interest in community capacity building (discussed in Chapter 2), rural managers have a high level of interface and a higher profile than might normally be expected of frontline supervisors within social work agencies (Lehmann, 2005). They enjoy few opportunities for peer support and discussion, and are often regarded by their urban-based colleagues as being somehow less responsible and deserving of attention because of direct size comparisons (Lehmann, 2005). In reality, however, rural managers are under constant scrutiny and judgement over every aspect of their lives, leading to caution about social outings, emotionally guarded behaviour and a reluctance to share feelings with others within their communities as news of perceived failings or weakness travels very quickly (Lehmann, 2005). Their role as managers with responsibility for staff recruitment, disciplinary and other management functions can also result in unreasonable judgement by fellow community members: as discussed in Chapter 2 in relation to confidentiality, misinformation is not easily corrected.

In Chapter 2 consideration was given to the skills required by social work practitioners in rural settings. These obviously apply to supervisors and managers also, but they additionally might be expected to demonstrate qualities such as organisational ability, resourcefulness, ability to facilitate and leadership. The need for such skills will arise from small local organisational infrastructure and geographical distance from other agency management representatives. Micek (2005) describes the particular skills in 'paucity management' used by community welfare managers and workers in the voluntary sector to address issues of resource poverty in remote rural settings in Australia. She characterises the managers she studied as having immense skill in 'navigation' and 'negation' within the boundaries presented by budget constraints, management and reporting structures, partnership arrangements, as well as governance guidelines and recommendations. Such 'limit-situations' are often turned from 'limitations' to 'opportunities' (2005, p. 301) by managers who work under a 'constant state of siege' (2005, p. 307). They must, she says 'be all things to all people and this requires a large amount of skill in generalist practice as well as a healthy dose of adaptability and flexibility' (2005, p. 306). Within the framework of managerialism described above, these are skills that are also found in the public sector. All this involves 'doing more with less' in order to 'transverse their situations of resource poverty into creative and innovative, manageable chunks of work' (2005, p. 308). Rural managers, it seems, are adept at creating opportunity out of adversity.

New technologies

The technological revolution of the past twenty years has created opportunities to address problems related to communication and geography that have been every bit as important and innovatory as the introduction of the telegraph in the nineteenth century. Systems have been developed that allow instant sharing of letters (emails), information, images, records and data over any distance. This book was written in a remote location without a single visit to a library, but with reasonably ready access to information sources thanks to a personal computer with internet availability. Technologies can facilitate the sharing of live moving images and, as noted in Chapter 4, the monitoring of vulnerable individuals through various telecare devices. All this reduces the isolation experienced in rural and remote places for service users and human services workers. Martinez-Brawley (2000), however, warns of the dangers of depersonalisation as this is introduced into personal services. In order to consider use in the rural context the commonly used technologies and their application (or potential) will be briefly examined in turn.

- The *world wide web* or *internet* is the basis of much of the new communication technology. Its use for sharing and finding information has opened up possibilities that were unavailable to remote and rural communities in the past. It really is now a case of knowing where to find information on the internet rather than whether it is there, and online resource websites for social workers (see end of chapter) usefully promote such use. Ife (2008) regards the internet as an empowering tool that has the potential (depending on how many people have access to it in the first place) to facilitate democracy and citizen participation. There are certainly examples of internet activity between people across the country and even the globe, influencing the actions of large organisations, whether over Christmas number one chart music, or (Ife's example) the multilateral agreement on investment in the 1990s. The internet is also the basis of client record and data systems that have aided the managerialist drive towards centralised control described earlier in this chapter. Harris (2003) warns that the surveillance and universality that such systems enable, become a means to their own end, driving the types of information recorded and reducing work to a series of technical tasks. However, online records are useful to workers who wish to access recording systems remotely although this remains an issue between partner agencies such as health and social services, sometimes through the use of different computerised recording systems. There is also an acknowledged need to develop information technology systems in health and social care for remote and rural areas to enable more robust communications that will enhance 'E Health' (NHS Scotland Remote and Rural Steering Group, 2007, p. 82).

- *Computerised assessment tools* for child protection and other purposes are also in the process of introduction. These can save time and energy but must not be allowed to dictate practice: I am advised that in parts of the US, child protection workers now take these into the homes of children on laptop computers in order to assess risk; if information is forthcoming that does not fit the programme, the assessment cannot proceed, and both worker and child at potential risk are left helpless (Martinez-Brawley, 2009). This has parallels with the introduction of call centres into social work in the UK, a development with possible attractions to planners for services to remotely located service users. Whilst telephone helpline services, such as the Samaritans, have their place, the use of computerised programmes to undertake social work assessments is quite a different type of service. Technical skill in the use of computerised technology cannot substitute for human decisions about the services required by individuals and such services will always have severe limitations (Coleman and Harris, 2008).

- *Emails* are generally regarded as a useful tool. They enable speedy written communication between individuals and groups with the advantage that these can be easily translated into recordings (subject to data protection laws and agency rules). Because they involve usually more consideration than telephone calls (that are necessarily more spontaneous), they can reflect thought-out positions, advice and guidance. On the other hand, if used without such consideration, they can record ill-considered expression in a way that telephone calls will not (unless recorded, which requires permission and is not routine). Rural workers report that they are useful for communication between busy individuals who are hard to access (Brownlee *et al.*, 2010). In my own work context, social workers find them useful for exchanging information with GPs, who can access them between seeing patients and respond quickly because they are less intrusive than telephone calls. The use of mobile telephone email access has increased this potential. They are, however, perhaps too easily shared: within an organisation all emails are the property of that organisation if sent from one of their computers; if that organisation, as many do, has its own intranet system with central computer servers, emails can be accessed without the permission of the sender or recipient. Caution needs to be exercised with their use and just as with other social work records, fact and opinion require to be clearly delineated, and gossip avoided.

- *Mobile telephones* have revolutionised communication. Subject to network availability (sometimes lacking in remote areas), workers can be contacted by colleagues, offices and support networks; in turn they can keep in touch, access information and engage in brokerage activity from a service user's home. As indicated in Chapter 2, this can go some way towards addressing health and safety concerns for staff working in isolated locations. However, mobile telephones increase the risk of intrusion, especially if they are carried all the time and never switched off. Workers who undertake out-of-hours duty might not have this option but otherwise proper appreciation of boundaries should dictate their hours of usage. Some staff choose not to give out their mobile telephone number to service users, whilst others encourage contact if this is part of the working contract (Chernowath and Stehlik, 2002). Text messaging might be considered a useful form of instant communication between staff within an agency, but might have limitations if used with service users. Discretion needs to be applied and the risk of intrusion properly considered.

- *Video conferencing* seems to be regarded as a useful means of audio visual contact when physical meeting is considered impractical. It can be used for individual meetings and group conferencing. Its success seems to depend on the reliability and scope of the technology involved (Chernoweth and Stehlik, 2002). As outlets become more available and the cost reduces this should be easier to access for all parties, but at present access might be an issue in disadvantaged communities where resources are limited (Wasko, 2005). The use of video conferencing is reported as decreasing the sense of isolation for remotely located staff working with difficult and demanding situations (Coholic and Blackford 2005); it has also been found to be effective for mental health services, including family therapy between patient and therapist in one location, and family in another (Wasko, 2005).

- *Home working* is now being introduced in public services to take advantage of communication technologies. It gives an opportunity for staff to work flexibly from home, with computer access to internet record systems with office support based elsewhere. Whilst some workers have welcomed this, it has implications for social services staff who work in situations of potential risk. It raises questions about safety, lone working, support and supervision. Whilst it might superficially lend itself as a cost-saving exercise to singleton staff who anyway work in remote situations, its use is not consistent with managing all the issues raised elsewhere in this chapter and Chapter 2.

In their recent research into the applicability of communication technologies in rural social work practice, Brownlee *et al.* (2010, p. 625) started from a premise that:

recent technological advances in telecommunications have the capacity for addressing many of the issues identified with rural and remote social work practice, such as the scarcity of professional resources, professional isolation and limited access to supervision and professional development.

They also contended that the distinction between rural and urban practice will reduce and that community-based generalist practice might be replaced by the type of specialist practice found in urban areas. They warned strongly, however, of the dangers of eroding the rural context of practice in line with the arguments made in Chapter 2 of this book. Warning should also be given about the manner in which new technologies can be used for surveillance and discipline of individual workers in line with the managerialist controlling agenda discussed earlier in this chapter; this might include monitoring of mobile telephone and internet use. As Weiner and Petrella (2007, p. 238) suggest, 'technology is neutral; it loses that neutrality when humans use technology for purposes that degrade, not improve, the quality of life, including the quality of work life'.

Rural social work commentators agree that face-to-face contact is still preferred over technologies in rural communities (Brownlee and Graham, 2005; Wasko, 2005) and care should be taken to ensure that workers do not hide behind technology in order to avoid necessary but potentially unpleasant direct contact (Chernowath and Stehlik, 2002). Wasko (2005) suggests that private sector market drivers will promote the increased use of technologies in the human services in the US, and as these form such an important part of the economy of other developed countries such as Scotland, the same argument will apply here. Their development will, however, depend on cost factors, access, security guarantees and user-friendliness.

Key summary points

- Organisational form will necessarily vary between local authorities and between localities, but needs to suit rural requirements rather than agency priorities.

- Supervision and workload management are as important in the rural and remote setting as they are anywhere else. Systems are required to ensure that they are in place for all staff, especially given the particular issues that arise from living and working in the same locality.

- Rurally based managers require particular generalist skills because of the leadership role they are likely to play in their communities that will go beyond that expected in an urban social work setting. These need to be acknowledged and given support by employing agencies.

- New technologies such as the internet and mobile telephones can be very useful in addressing problems relating to professional isolation. They are not, however, developed enough to replace face-to-face communication between service users and social workers.

Recommended further reading and online resources

Jennifer Lehmann's paper is particularly useful (even though written from an Australian perspective) as it describes pressures on rural managers that are recognisable in the Scottish context. The paper by Brownlee et al. provides a useful summary of the possibilities and problems with new technologies.

Brownlee, K, Graham, J, Doucette, E, Hotson, N and Halverson, G (2010) 'Have communication technologies influenced rural social work practice?' *British Journal of Social Work* **40(1)** pp. 622-37.

Lehmann, J (2005) 'Human services management in rural contexts' *British Journal of Social Work* **35(3)** pp. 355-71.

Those looking for an extensive online social work information resource in Scotland need look no further than the Social Service Knowledge Scotland (SSKS) website: www.ssks.org.uk/home.aspx

Chapter 7

Conclusions: Does Rural Social Work in Scotland have a Future?

Introduction

This final chapter of the book features a case study involving two perspectives on a fairly typical referral in a remote rural area. One involves social work assessment and service delivery from a social worker from a locally based team, and the other from a worker approaching the issues from outside the community. Both are necessarily kept as simple as possible as it would be superfluous to go into too much organisational detail about what are essentially imaginary scenarios.

The H family

Mr and Mrs H have moved from a city in the West of Scotland onto the island of Erismay, which is a 45-minute ferry journey from the West Coast seaport of Fishton. Fishton, with a population of 25,000 people, is the largest town within an 80-mile radius and has an array of shops, facilities and local authority service bases. Erismay, with a population of 3,000 people, consists of a scattering of villages around its 75-mile coastline, with one larger settlement where the ferries arrive from Fishton, and it is here that the largest shops, the bank and the main post office are situated.

The H's consist of Mr and Mrs H, their 15-year-old daughter Amy, their

12-year-old son Arnold, and Mr H's widowed mother who is in her early eighties. Mr H formerly worked for a large motor retailer as a mechanic. He can turn his hand to a variety of practical tasks and would like to make a living on Erismay through self-employment as a handyman. Mrs H suffers from depression, one of the reasons why the family decided to move to a place they had enjoyed for holidays. They have borrowed heavily to finance the move from their council house in the city to a privately rented house on Erismay. Mrs H senior has lived with the family for about two years and suffers from short-term memory and mobility problems. The family had no dealings with social services where they previously lived.

Take one

Carol is a qualified social worker and practice team leader who works full time in the Erismay Council office, along with Judith, a qualified social worker and two social work assistants, Bob and Morag. The office is also the location of a part-time occupational therapist (OT) Joanne, whose duties encompass social work as well as health referrals via the Erismay community hospital (her post is jointly funded by the council and the health authority), and two part-time care-at-home service organisers. The office is shared with other council services and is very near the police office, the high school, the community hospital and the office of the island Council of Voluntary Service. The social work team operate generically: Carol and Judith have a mixed workload of community care, and children and family cases, whilst the two social work assistants tend to work mainly (but not exclusively) with community care cases. The two social workers, the two social work assistants and the OT operate a fairly informal duty system whereby each stays in the office one day a week to take new referrals. Carol has supervision responsibilities for all the staff and is herself managed from the Fishton office on the mainland. Carol and all the other Erismay staff are experienced: both she and Judith have completed post-graduate diploma courses in child protection; Judith is also a mental health officer. Whilst

Carol, Judith and Joanne originate from the mainland, Bob and Morag are native islanders.

Carol attends regular multi-professional partnership meetings with colleagues in education and health that were initiated under the *Getting It Right For Every Child* (GIRFEC) Agenda. At one of these on 27 May 2009, she heard concerns from the high school guidance staff about Amy H. Apparently, Amy, who only started at the school some six months previously, has poor attendance and has taken up with a small group of unemployed school leavers who spend much of their time drinking alcohol and smoking cannabis. Within the school she has been in trouble for fighting with other girls and confrontation with certain teachers in the classroom setting. The meeting had concluded that with the parents' permission, a referral to social services for some informal advice seemed appropriate, and that this would give opportunity for further assessment of the situation at home. Carol checked with the computerised record system and saw that her colleague Joanne the OT had been involved briefly soon after the family move to Erismay, with Mrs H senior, and had arranged for the supply of some small aids. Joanne had noted some concern that the family did not seem to be awake to the realities of life in their new community, such as the dearth of facilities, and that there were tensions around this. Joanne confirmed this when Carol spoke to her informally about the family. Joanne had also had concerns about the state of the tenancy generally – an address well known to social services for the succession of families that had passed through whilst awaiting social housing, of which there was a shortage.

The parents advised the school that they were happy to see a social worker, admitting that they were at the end of their tether with Amy. Carol called at the home by appointment when both parents and Amy could be present. She identified a number of issues concerning not just Amy, but also Mrs H, Mrs H senior, and income and debt issues affecting them all. As a result of this she began to work out a plan of action with the family that resulted in discussions with other involved agencies: the high school, the youth service, the GP and the social housing provider. This also involved assessment and services for Mrs H senior. All of these agencies and the individuals who worked in them, the various services they provided and the resources available to them, were well known to Carol.

Although Amy was quite unsettled by her move to Erismay, she began to engage with a mentor arranged by Carol, and work out a plan for herself. There was a referral from the police to the reporter to the Children's Panel after an incident involving alcohol, but by then Amy was working with the mentor on a voluntary basis. Later, having received information from social services, the reporter agreed to take no further action.

Take two

The Fishton social work office covers a large West Highland area including several offshore islands reached by ferry journeys of various lengths. Often in winter, services to these islands are disrupted by the weather, and social work visits, usually conducted on particular days of the week, involve long days. Fishton social work office is divided into two distinct teams: a children and family team who are part of the council's children's services department, and the community care team who are part of the council's housing and community service department. The two are therefore managed entirely separately but are in regular liaison on a local basis when cases are transferred between them. This can lead to tensions about the borders of responsibility but staff all work in the same office and get on well together on a personal basis. The community care team have some social work assistants based on the outlying islands, including two on the Isle of Erismay. They and a locally based care-at-home organiser tend to deal with the more routine work in connection with the island's large older population. The Fishton office deals with all new referrals: adults to the community care team and children and family matters to the children and family team.

Jim is a social worker in the children and family team in Fishton. He is an experienced children and family worker with a post-graduate qualification in child protection, and previous experience of work in a large city setting.

Most of Jim's work is in the Fishton area, but he spends a lot of time travelling to the outlying parts of the patch, and this can be problematic in the winter with appointments often cancelled or delayed.

On 7 October, Jim was allocated a report on Amy H following referral from the children's reporter. This related to an alcohol-related breach of the peace that had come to the attention of the police on Erismay. As is normal under local GIRFEC procedures, Jim arranged to discuss Amy's situation at the next Erismay multi-agency children's forum in three weeks' time. Because the social work children and family service for Erismay is only available for 'tier two and three' referrals (see Figure 2.1, Chapter 2), the purpose of the multi-agency forum is to scrutinise all referrals from the reporter, as well as other high-risk situations. Jim meantime checked the computerised record system and saw that there was only one referral to an OT in housing and community care services some ten months previously. This was of no great interest to Jim as it concerned an 81-year-old woman who might be Amy's grandmother. Anyway, he would find out more when he visited the family. When he has to go to Erismay Jim visits on a Thursday, and managed to get the family on the telephone and arrange a home visit the following week. This would have to be as soon as Amy came home from school at 4.20pm, as the last ferry left the island at 6.00pm. This would mean that he would not be able to meet Mr H who has work at that time on a Thursday, which he could not afford to forgo. The multi-agency forum would take place two weeks later.

Jim's visit to the family identified a number of worries and concerns. The house was damp and in poor condition and the rent seemed very high. Amy was angry with her mother and father for the family's move to Erismay and her presentation and the descriptions of her behaviour were concerning. Mrs H seemed to be very isolated and barely coping with anything; she suggested that Amy should be removed from home as she was out of control. There were also tensions around having to look after her elderly mother-in-law. Mr H's views were not known but he was said to be out a great deal in his efforts to earn enough to meet the family's debts. Jim suggested that contact should be made with the Citizens Advice Bureau about debt and housing issues, and agreed to refer to the community care team in Fishton for assistance in relation to Mrs H senior. He also suggested that Mrs H should go to see her GP about her depression although she said she was already on medication.

When Jim attended the multi-agency forum a week later he gathered more concerns about Amy and her family. A teacher present believed that the police were regular visitors to the home. There was agreement that Amy should go to a Children's Hearing with a recommendation for a Supervision Order, but some pessimism that this would not be enough to prevent her situation from escalating.

The different approaches to intervention with the H family

There are a number of issues (discussed in earlier chapters of this book) described above that will be familiar scenarios to social workers who practice in rural areas regardless of their team setting:

- the impact of change from an urban to a remote rural setting on young people who may not have bought into a family decision to move;
- alcohol and its place in rural society and impact on young people;
- the alienation experienced by disadvantaged young people in remote rural areas;
- issues relating to poor standards of housing, social housing scarcity and high living costs;
- the precarious nature of self-employment/employment in a remote rural area;
- the impact of caring for a dependent elderly family member in a situation of relative isolation;
- issues relating to mental health and the expectation that some people have that a move to a rural setting might provide solutions to problems they experienced in an urban setting.

The way in which problems are identified, and assistance and support offered, differs between the two models described. Carol is based in the locality and works closely with colleagues in other partner agencies. This leads to early identification of emerging issues with the family and a plan based on knowledge of the context, the networks and resources available. She does not necessarily need to refer social work assessment matters on to other colleagues, and if she does they will be people she works with closely and can liaise with easily. Jim, on the other hand, despite his skills and experience, is only able to become involved when matters have reached a point of statutory referral for Amy. His focus then is on her needs and he has to refer other aspects of the family's problems on to others. His liaison with other involved agencies may not involve good working relationships based on mutual dependence, but may be more formalised, depending for example, on the multi-agency GIRFEC-inspired forum. Covering such a wide area, it cannot be assumed that he has a particular knowledge of Erismay as a community or understanding of the issues facing the H family. He is instead likely to apply his social work knowledge of children and family issues and whilst this may well lead to good outcomes for Amy, it may not be able to bring strategies to bear that will help prevent her situation from escalating. Any work plan involving Jim or other mainland-based specialist staff is likely to be disrupted by weather issues and limited by travel options. The brief description of the two team models suggests that Carol's setting involves local staff with local knowledge that will enhance what she already knows and understands from her own place in the community. She is likely to have a close working relationship with the police, education staff and others mentioned that will help the family deal with the issues they face. Jim may have a contact on Erismay who can guide him with some of the rural context issues but this may be problematic. These two case scenarios are not intended to be particularly dichotomous. In reality, differences in response and service may even be more diverse than in this example, especially if the mainland children and family team are under pressure (as most are). There are of course numerous service delivery models but these two are considered fairly typical ones. The argument here is that a community-based service offers a great deal of additionality to a social work service that will more than compensate for the costs involved.

Final words

Even with the contraction of public services engendered by the spending crisis, it seems unlikely that the place of social work in rural and remote Scotland is endangered. This book has evidenced and argued throughout that there are particular considerations that require different skills in a rural and remote setting. These considerations and skills can be summarised as:

- understanding the locality: its geography, history, cultural profile, minority groups, networks and leaders;
- adapting to living and working in the same community, including appreciation of initial acceptance issues, dual relationship issues, confidentiality issues and working in relative professional isolation;
- whether a specialist or generic social worker, utilising generalist skills to work across boundaries and find the best solutions to the problems of service users: this will require knowledge of policy as well as funding mechanisms and opportunities;
- using community-orientated, collective approaches as well as more traditional individual casework methods of practice.

Social work models and organisational forms that are based entirely on urban practice ignore these variations and do social workers who practice in rural and remote localities, and the service users they care for, a disservice. In Australia and Canada, where such issues are discussed more widely and addressed in at least some professional training courses (Pugh and Cheers, 2010), the blurring of such difference has been blamed for high turnover and staff retention problems (Lonne and Cheers, 2000; Schmidt, 2000). There is no research to indicate whether these are problems in

Scotland but it can be assumed that a failure to address rural social work issues can only have negative impact on workers and their supervisors. If there is such a failure in Scotland it should not be surprising when one considers that there is no formal attention to rural issues on any professional social work training degree courses. However, there is interest in rural social work themes in Scottish universities, as evidenced by a straw poll undertaken by the author when this book was in its very earliest stages of preparation. Small-scale local training initiatives on rural themes (as undertaken in my own setting) have been received well and could be extended through more developed packages. All that gives some hope for the future, as does the growing volume of well-researched international literature on the subject, much of which has been quoted in this book. It is hoped, too, that this volume will give some impetus to further such study and initiative in Scotland.

Despite this optimism there are trends internationally that are pushing social work as a profession into managerially controlled, narrowly confined and specialised service models to the detriment of rural social work (Murty, 2005). Olive Stevenson (2005, p. 581) voices a parallel argument about the general trajectory of social work in the UK:

In my view social work has been blown off course. It has been argued that for a variety of reasons, some internal and some external to the profession, social work has failed to establish the two interrelated aspects of its identity – a clearly delineated generic foundation upon which specialisms that have professional and intellectual coherence could be built.

Whilst Stevenson is not necessarily arguing here for community-orientated and more contextually based practice, she is suggesting where the root of the problem lies. In this sense the issues are as important for urban-based as they are for rural-based social workers. At its heart, social work is about relationship building with service users and carers based on respect and non-judgemental attitudes, and then joint work around strategies to address problems (Ferguson and Woodward, 2009). Rural- and remotely-based workers, because they find themselves working in situations where they are reliant on knowledge of local communities (Pugh and Cheers, 2010), are in an advantageous position to build such relationships and work to the values and ideals that probably brought them into social work. These are under threat because of general trends internationally as well as in the UK context (Harris, 1999; Harris, 2003; McDonald, 2006; Ferguson and Woodward, 2009). Such trends, discussed throughout this book, present a threat to the type of community-orientated generalist practice (described in Chapter 2) that fits rural and remote communities. Already in Scotland there are signs of such encroachment on social work services in rural and remote areas, with organisational form and working arrangements differing little to that found in Scotland's cities. Whether the erasure of generalist forms is a response to perceptions of practice deficit, as has perhaps been the case in Eilean Siar, or because of centrally driven policy directives and inspection regimes, social workers might find themselves at a disadvantage in arguing for alternatives if there is little understanding of what these might be, and what they are based on. It is also contended that the development of communication technology, (discussed in Chapter 6) might also erode rural-urban difference in social work practice (Brownlee et al., 2010). However, the breaking down of isolation through improved audio, audio-visual and written communication technologies will not address the contextual and relationship issues listed at the start of this chapter that are the basis of rural social work practice.

This book has argued throughout that social work in the remote and rural areas of Scotland is at least as challenging as practice in the cities. It has the potential to be rewarding and innovative, and to make a contribution to rural life in keeping with the aspirations laid down for the profession within the pages of Changing Lives (Scottish Executive, 2006). This will not happen by itself, but can be realised through the efforts of practitioners and those who train them.

References

Adams, R, Dominelli, L and Payne, M (2002) *Social Work: Themes, issues and critical debates* Basingstoke: Palgrave Macmillan.

Anderson, S (1998) *A Study of Crime in Rural Scotland* Edinburgh: The Stationery Office.

Arbuthnott, J (2009) *Clyde Valley Review 09*, Renfrewshire: Renfrewshire Council, www.renfrewshire.gov.uk/ilwwcm/publishing.nsf/Content/ce-gm-features-ClydeValleyReview

Association of Directors of Social Work (2005) 'Context for 21st Century Social Work: Social Work 1968-21st Century' Paper submitted to the *Scottish 21st Century Review of Social Work*.

Asthana, S and Gibson, A, Monn, G and Brigham, P (2003) 'Allocating Resources for Health and Social Care: the Significance of Rurality.' *Health and Social Care in the Community*, **11(6)**, pp. 486-93.

Audit Scotland (2009) *Scotland's Public Finances – Preparing for the Future,* November, Edinburgh: Audit Scotland, www.audit-scotland.gov.uk

Bailey, N, Spratt, J, Pickering, J, Goodlad, R and Shucksmith, M (2004) *Deprivation and Social Exclusion in Argyll and Bute – Report to the Community Planning Partnership*, Glasgow: Scottish Centre for Research on Social Justice, Universities of Glasgow and Aberdeen.

Barnes, M (1997) *Care, Communities and Citizens* Harlow, Essex: Longman.

BBC News (2004) 'History Spurs Anti-English Tirade', 12 July, http://news.bbc.co.uk/1/hi/scotland/3886381.stm

BBC News (2005) 'Gypsy Campaign Raises Ethics Issues', 11 March, http://news.bbc.co.uk/2/hi/uk_news/4337281.stm

BBC News (2009) 'Free Personal Care Costs in Scotland Rise by 11%', 24 November, http://news.bbc.co.uk/1/hi/scotland/8376819.stm

BBC News Highland (2008) 'Rural Post Offices to be Closed', 8 January, http://news.bbc.co.uk/1/hi/scotland/highlands_and_islands/7175567.stm

BBC News Scotland (1999) 'Suicide Risk of Highland Men', 2 November, http://news.bbc.co.uk/1/hi/scotland/502229.stm

Beyond Barriers (2004) *Linking Scotland, Planning Futures: Report of Beyond Barriers National Conference on the Needs of LGBT People in Rural and Remote Scotland,* Glasgow: Beyond Barriers.

Bornat, J, Pereira, C, Pilgrim, D and Williams, F (eds) (1993) *Community Care: A Reader* Basingstoke: Macmillan.

Boyd, C and Parr, H (2008) 'Commentary: Social Geography and Rural Mental Health Research' *Rural and Remote Health* **8:804** [online], www.rrh.org.au

Breitenbach, E and Wassof, F (2007) *A Gender Audit of Statistics: Comparing the Position of Women and Men in Scotland,* Edinburgh: Scottish Executive Social Research, www.scotland.gov.uk/Publications/2007/03/27104103/0

Brody, S (2009) 'Salmond Stands Up For Social Workers' *Community Care,* 6 March.

Bromley, C, Curtice, J and Given, L (2007) *Attitudes to Discrimination in Scotland 2006: Scottish Social Attitudes Survey,* Edinburgh: Scottish Centre for Social Research, www.scotland.gov.uk/Resource/Doc/205755/0054714.pdf

Brown, J (1933) *The Rural Community and Social Case Work,* New York: Family Welfare Association of America.

Brownlee, K and Graham, K (eds) (2005) *Violence in the Family: Social Work Readings and Research from Northern and Rural Canada* Toronto: CSPI.

Brownlee, K, Graham, J, Doucette, E, Hotson, N and Halverson, G (2010) 'Have Communication Technologies Influenced Rural Social Work Practice?' *British Journal of Social Work* **40(1)** pp. 622-37.

Bruce, S, Hume, D and Jay A (eds) (2009) *Creating Positive Outcomes Through Social Work Service* London: SOLACE Foundation and the Scottish Government, www.solace.org.uk/library_documents/ SFI_Creating_positive_outcomes_through_social_work_practices.pdf

Burke, B and Harrison, P (2002) 'Anti-Oppressive Practice' in Adams, R, Dominelli, L and Payne, M *Social Work: Themes, Issues and Critical Debates* (2nd edition), Basingstoke: Palgrave.

Cemlyn, S (2008) 'Human Rights and Gypsy Travellers: An Exploration of the Application of a Human Rights Perspective to Social Work with a Minority Community in Britain' *British Journal of Social Work* **38(1)** pp. 153-73.

Cemlyn, S, Greenfields, M, Burnett, S, Matthews, Z and Whitwell, C (2009) *Inequalities Experienced by Gypsy and Traveller Communities: A Review* Manchester: Equality and Human Rights Commission.

Cheers, B (1998) *Welfare Bushed: Social Care in Rural Australia*, Aldershot: Ashgate.

Cheers, B, Darracott, R and Lonne, B (2005) 'Domains of Rural Social Work Practice' *Rural Society* **15(2)**, pp. 234-51.

Cheers, B, Darracott, R and Lonne, B (2007) *Social Care Practice in Rural Communities* Sydney: The Federation Press.

Chernowath, L and Stehlik, D (2002) 'Using Technology in Rural Practice – Local Area Coordination in Rural Australia' *Rural Social Work*, **7(1)** pp. 14-21.

Clark, C (2006) 'Defining Ethnicity in a Cultural and Socio-Legal Context: The Case of Scottish Gypsy-Travellers' *Scottish Affairs*, **54**, pp. 39-67.

Cloke, P, Milbourne, P and Widdowfield, R (2002) *Rural Homelessness: Issues, Experiences and Policy Responses* Bristol: The Policy Press.

Clyde, Lord (1992) *The Report of the Inquiry into the Removal of Children from Orkney in February 1991* Edinburgh: HMSO.

Coholic, D and Blackford, K 'Exploring Secondary Trauma in Sexual Assault Workers in Northern Ontario Locations' in Brownlee, K and Graham, J (eds) *Violence in the Family: Social Work Readings and*

Research from Northern and Rural Canada Toronto: CSPI.

Coleman, N and Harris, J (2008) 'Calling Social Work' *British Journal of Social Work*, **38(3)**, pp. 580-99.

Collier, K. (2006) *Social Work with Rural Peoples* (3rd edition), Vancouver: New Star.

Commission for Rural Communities (2006) *Rural Disadvantage: Reviewing the Evidence* London: Countryside Agency.

Communities Scotland (2005) 'The impact of second and holiday homes on rural communities in Scotland' *PRECiS*, 70, www.scotland.gov.uk/Resource/Doc/1125/0086619.pdf

Communities Scotland (2006) *Services for Gypsies/Travellers: A Follow Up Study 2005/06* Edinburgh: Regulation and Inspection Section, Communities Scotland.

Coulshed, V and Mullender, A (2006) *Management in Social Work* (3rd edition), Basingstoke: Palgrave Macmillan.

Craig, G and Manthorpe, J (2000) *Fresh Fields: Rural Social Care: Research, Policy and Practice Agendas* York: Joseph Rowntree Foundation.

CRE (Commission for Racial Equality) (2005) *Gypsies and Travellers: A Draft Strategy for the CRE in Scotland, 2005-2007*, Edinburgh: CRE Scotland, www.srec.org.uk/srec_reports_download.asp?id=17

Dawson, R (2007) *Empty Lands: Aspects of Scottish Gypsy and Traveller Survival* Alfreton Derbys: Dawson.

de Lima, P (2005) *Addressing Racial Harrassment in Rural Communities*, 18 August, www.cjscotland.org.uk/index.php/cjscotland/ dynamic_page/?title=racial_harrassment

Denton, R and Denton M (1998) 'Treating Religious Fundamentalist Families: Therapists' Suggestions from a Qualitative Study' in Ginsberg L (ed) *Social Work in Rural Communities* Alexandria, CA: CSWE.

Dominelli, L (2007) 'Human Rights in Social Work Practice: An Invisible Part of the Social Work Curriculum?' in Reichart, E (ed) *Challenges in*

Human Rights: A Social Work Perspective, New York: Columbia University Press.

Drillsma-Millgrom, D (2009) 'Two tier attack may be sign of things to come', www.lgcplus.com/blogs/two-tier-attack-could-be-sign-of-times-to-come/5004856.blog

Ellen Welsh, M (1995) 'Rural Social Work Practice – Clinical Quality' in Compton, B and Galway, B (eds) *Social Work Processes* (5th edition), Pacific Grove, CA: Brooks Cole.

England, H (1986) *Social Work as Art*, London: Allen and Unwin.

European Network for Indigenous Australian Rights News (undated) 'People of Shetland unite to save failed asylum-seekers from deportation', www.eniar.org/news/Koolmatrie.html

Evans, T and Harris, J (2004) 'Street-Level Bureaucracy, Social Work and the (Exaggerated) Death of Discretion' *British Journal of Social Work* **34(6)** pp. 871-95.

Evening Times Glasgow (2006) *Demo Over Care Home Closure*, 10 January.

Ferguson, I (2007) 'Increasing User Choice or Privatising Risk: The Antinomies of Personalisation' *British Journal of Social Work* **37(3)** pp. 387-403.

Ferguson, I & Woodward, R (2009) *Radical Social Work in Practice – Making a Difference* Bristol: The Policy Press.

Galbreath, W (2005) 'Dual Relationships in Rural Communities' in Lohmann, N and Lohmann, R (eds) *Rural Social Practice*, New York: Columbia University Press.

Ginsberg, L (ed) (1998) *Social Work in Rural Communities* (3rd edition) Alexandria, VA: CSWE.

Ginsberg, L (1998b) 'Introduction: An Overview of Rural Social Work.' in Ginsberg, L (ed) (1998) *Social Work in Rural Communities* (3rd edition), Alexandria, VA: CSWE.

Glendinning, A, Nuttal, M, Hendry, L, Kloep, M and Wood, S (2003) 'Rural Communities and Well-Being: a Good Place to Grow Up?' *Sociological*

Review **51(1)**, pp. 129-56.

Grayling, A C (2008) *Social Evils and Social Good* York: Joseph Rowntree Foundation, www.jrf.org.uk/sites/files/jrf/2281.pdf

Green, R and Mason, R (2002) 'Managing Confidentiality in Rural Welfare Practice in Australia' *Rural Social Work* **7(1)**, pp. 34-43.

Green, R G (1989) 'The Badenoch and Strathspey Social Work Team' in Smale, G & Bennett, T (eds) *Community Social Work in Scotland: Pictures of Practice Vol 1* London: PADE.

Green, R G (1993) 'From Survival Planning to Proactive Practice' in Martinez-Brawley, E & Delevan, S (eds) *Transferring Technology in the Personal Social Services,* Washington: NASW Press.

Griffiths, R (1988) *Community Care: Agenda for action* London: HMSO.

GROS (General Register Office for Scotland) (2005, revised 2007) '2004-based Population Projections for Scottish Areas', www.gro-scotland.gov.uk/statistics/publications-and-data/popproj/04pop-proj-scottishareas/index.html

Hadley, R, Cooper, M, Dale, P and Stacey, G (1987) *A Community Social Worker's Handbook* London: Tavistock Publications.

Handon, R (2009) 'Client Relationships and Ethical Boundaries for Social Workers in Child Welfare' *The New Social Worker* [Online] www.socialworker.com/home/Feature_Articles/Ethics/Client_Relationships_and_Ethical_Boundaries_for_Social_Workers_in_Child_Welfare/

Harris, J (1999) 'Social Work Sent to Market' *International Perspectives in Social Work: Social Work and the State* Brighton: Pavilion.

Harris, J (2003) *The Social Work Business* London: Routledge.

Harris, J (2007) 'Looking Backward, Looking Forward: Current Trends in Human Services Management' in Aldgate, J, Healy, L, Malcolm, B, Pine, B, Rose, W and Seden, J (eds) *Enhancing Social Work Management: Theory and Best Practice from the UK and USA,* London: Jessica Kingsley Publishers.

Hawthorn, J (2009) *Significant Case Review: Brandon Lee Muir* Edinburgh: Scottish Police Services Authority.

Hothersall, S (2008) *Social Work with Children, Young People and their Families in Scotland* (2nd edition), Exeter: Learning Matters.

House of Commons (2008) Hansard Debates, 30 January, www.publications.parliament.uk/pa/cm200708/cmhansrd/cm080130/debtext/80130-0023.htm

Horwarth, J and Lees, J (2010) 'Assessing the Influence of Religious Beliefs and Practices on Parenting Capacity: The Challenges for Social Work Practitioners' *British Journal of Social Work* **40(1)**, pp. 82-99.

Howard League for Penal Reform (2005), *Once Upon a Time in the West: Social Deprivation and Rural Youth Crime*, London, Howard League for Penal Reform.

Hudson, B (2008) *Supporting People in Remote and Rural Areas: A Framework for Analysis*, Edinburgh: Health Scotland Joint Improvement Team, Remote and Rural Implementation Group, www.jitscotland.org.uk/action-areas/rural-and-remote/publications/

Hunter, J (1994) *A Dance Called America: The Scottish Highlands, The United States and Canada*, Edinburgh: Mainstream.

Ife, J (2008) *Human Rights and Social Work: Towards Rights-Based Practice* (2nd edition) Cambridge: Cambridge University Press.

Independent on Sunday (2006) *Local hero:* 'Shetland islanders celebrate as Thai man caught up in foreign prisoners row beats deportation threat and wins his right to stay', 8 July, www.independent.co.uk/news/uk/crime/local-hero-shetland-islanders-celebrate-as-thai-man-caught-up-in-foreign-prisoners-row-beats-deportation-threat-and-wins-his-right-to-stay-407088.html

IFSW (International Federation of Social Workers) (2004) *Ethics in Social Work: Statement of Principles*, Berne, Switzerland: IFSW, www.ifsw.org/f38000032.html

Inverness Courier (2007) 'U Turn Ends Private Threat to Care Homes', 15 June.

Irvine Herald (2008a) 'Travellers Branded Anarchists by MP', 25 January.

Irvine Herald (2008b) 'New Approach Needed for Travellers – MP', 22 August.

Johnson, C (2009) 'An Evaluation of the Challenges Implicit for Social Workers Practicing in Remote Communities: A Focus on the Western Isles', Unpublished dissertation, Aberdeen: The Robert Gordon University.

Jones, C (2001) 'Voices from the Front Line: State Social Workers and New Labour' *British Journal of Social Work* **31(4)** pp. 547-62.

Joseph Rowntree Foundation (2009), *Social Evils' and 'Social Problems' in Britain 1904-2008'*, York: Joseph Rowntree Foundation, www.jrf.org.uk/sites/files/jrf/evils-social-problems.pdf

Kendrick, A and Rioch, C (1995), 'Knowing the Back Roads - Rural Social Work with Troubled Young People' *Youth and Policy* **51**, pp. 46-57.

Kerr, M (2003) *Bid 79: Recommendations for the safe management of acutely disturbed psychiatric patients in Scotland's remote and rural areas: Report of a consultation sponsored by RARARI,* Edinburgh: Scottish Executive.

King, D, Pashley, M and Ball, R (2007) 'Scotland's Social Services Spending Needs: An English View' *Environment and Planning C: Government and Policy*, **25(6)** pp. 918-40.

Krieg Mayer, A (2001) 'Rural Social Work: the Perceptions and Experiences of Five Remote Practitioners' *Australian Social Work,* **54**, pp. 91-102.

Laine Scales, T and Streeter, C (eds) (2004) *Rural Social Work: Building and Sustaining Community Assets*, Belmont CA: Thomson Brooks Cole.

Laming, Lord (2003) *The Victoria Climbié Inquiry* Norwich: HMSO.

Leadbeater, C (2004) *Personalisation Through Participation: A New Script for Public Services*, London: DEMOS.

Leadbeater, C and Lownsbrough, H (2005) *Personalisation and Participation: The Future of Social Care in Scotland,* London: DEMOS,

www.socialworkscotland.org.uk/resources/cp-sd/
PersonalisationThroughParticipationReport.pdf

Lehmann, J (2005) 'Human Services Management in Rural Contexts'
British Journal of Social Work **35(3)**, pp. 355-71.

Lipsky, M (1980) *Street-Level Bureaucracy: Dilemmas of the Individual in
Public Services,* New York: Russell Sage.

Locke, B and Winship, J (2005) 'Social Work in Rural America: Lessons
From the Past and Trends for the Future' in Lohmann, N and Lohmann,
R (eds) *Rural Social Work Practice* New York: Columbia University
Press.

Lohmann, N and Lohmann, R (eds) (2005a) *Rural Social Work Practice*,
New York: Columbia University Press.

Lohmann, N and Lohmann, R (2005b) 'What is Rural Practice' in
Lohmann, N and Lohmann, R (eds) *Rural Social Work Practice*, New
York: Columbia University Press.

London Borough of Brent (1985) *A Child in Trust: The Report of the Panel
of Inquiry into the Circumstances Surrounding the Death of Jasmine
Beckford* London: London Borough of Brent.

Lonne, B and Cheers, B (2000) 'Rural Social Workers and their Jobs: An
Empirical Study.' *Australian Social Work* **53(1)**, pp. 21-8.

Manthorpe, J and Livsey, L (2009) 'European Challenges in Delivering
Social Services in Rural Regions: a Scoping Review' *European Journal
of Social Work* **12(1)**, pp. 5-24.

Manthorpe, J and Stevens, M (2009) 'Increasing Care Options in the
Countryside: developing an Understanding of the Potential Impact of
Personalisation for Social Work with Rural Older People' *British Journal
of Social Work,* Advance Access: doi:10.1093/bjsw/bcp038.

Martinez-Brawley, E (1984) 'In Search of Common Principles in Rural
Social and Community Work' in Lishman, J (ed) *Social Work in Rural
and Urban Areas* Aberdeen: University of Aberdeen.

Martinez-Brawley, E (1986) 'Community-orientated Social Work in a Rural
and Remote Hebridean Patch' *International Social Work* **29** pp. 349-72.

Martinez-Brawley, E (1990) *Perspectives on the Small Community* Washington DC: NASW Press.

Martinez-Brawley, E (1998) 'Community-Orientated Practice in Rural Social Work' in Ginsberg, L (ed) *Social Work in Rural Communities* (3rd edition), Alexandria VA: CSWE.

Martinez-Brawley, E (2000), *Close to Home: Human Services and the Small Community*, Washington DC: NASW Press.

Martinez-Brawley, E (2009) personal communication.

Marx, K (1867) *Capital Volume 1,* www.marxists.org/archive/marx/works/1867

Mason, R (2006) 'Providing Social Care Services in Rural Australia: A Review' *Rural Social Work and Community Practice* **11**, December, pp. 40-51.

McCarry, M And Williamson, E (2009) *Violence Against Women in Rural and Urban Areas – Research Commissioned by the National Federation of Women's Institutes* Bristol: University of Bristol.

McDonald, C (2006) *Challenging Social Work: The Context of Practice* Basingstoke: Palgrave Macmillan.

McNeill, F and Whyte, B (2007) *Reducing Reoffending: Social Work and Community Justice in Scotland* Cullompton, Devon: Willan.

McVie, S (2008) *Rural Crime in Scotland: What Can We Learn From the Scottish Crime Survey and Scottish Neighbourhood Statistics?* Presentation to the SIPR conference, Inverness, May, www.sipr.ac.uk/downloads/Rural%crime%20Scotland.pps

Mermelstein, J (1991) 'Feminist Practice in Rural Social Work' in Bricker-Jenkins, M, Hooyman, N and Gottlieb, N (eds) *Feminist Social Work Practice in Clinical Settings*, Newbury Park, CA: Sage.

Micek, S (2005) 'Paucity Management Addresses the Limit-situations of Human Services Delivery in Rural Australia' *Rural Society* **15(3)** pp. 297-311.

Midwinter, A (2006) *Spending Review 2007: An Assessment of Expenditure Need by Scottish Local Authorities on Children's Social Work Services from 2007-2011*, Edinburgh: ADSW.

Miller, P. (1998) 'Dual Relationships in Rural Practice: A Dilemma of Ethics and Culture' in Ginsberg, L (ed) *Social Work in Rural Communities* (3rd edition), Alexandria VA: CSWE.

Morran, D (2002) 'Negotiating Marginalised Identities: Social Workers and Settled Travelling People in Scotland' *International Social Work* **45(3)** pp. 337-51.

Morris, R. (2000) 'Gypsies, Travellers and the Media: Press Regulation and Racism in the UK' *Communications Law* **5(6)** pp. 213-19.

Munro, E (2002) *Effective Child Protection*, London: Sage Publications.

Munro, N (1942) *Para Handy and other* tales (5th impression), Glasgow: Blackwood.

Murty, S (2005) 'The Future of Rural Social Work' *Advances in Social Work* **6(1)** pp. 132-44.

National Census (2001):
www.statistics.gov.uk/STATBASE/Expodata/Spreadsheets/D5966.xls

National Resource Centre for Ethnic Minority Health (2006) *Voices from the North: Explanatory Needs Assessment of Gypsy/Traveller Communities in the North of Scotland* Glasgow: National Resource Centre for Ethnic Minority Health.

Neate, T (1996) *The Summer Walkers: Travelling People and Pearl-Fishers in the Highlands of Scotland* Edinburgh: Canongate.

Netto, G, Arshad, R, de Lima, P, Almeida Diniz, F, MacEwan, M, Patel, V and Syed, R (2001) *Audit of Research on Minority Ethnic Issues in Scotland from a 'Race' Perspective* Edinburgh: Scottish Executive Central Research Unit.

Netto, G (2008) 'Multiculturalism in the Devolved Context: Minority Ethnic Negotiation of Identity Through Engagement in the Arts in Scotland' *Sociology* **42(1)** pp. 47-64.

NFU Scotland (2010) *Farming Facts*, Ingliston: NFU Scotland, www.nfus.org.uk/farming-facts

NHS Scotland (2009a) *Alcohol Statistics Scotland 2009* Edinburgh: ISD Publications.

NHS Scotland (2009b) *Shifting the Balance of Care* Edinburgh, NHS Scotland, www.shiftingthebalance.scot.nhs.uk/

NHS Scotland Remote and Rural Steering Group (2007) *Delivering for Remote and Rural Health Care: The Final Report of the Remote and Rural Workstream* Edinburgh: Scottish Government.

North Ayrshire Council (2007) *Isle of Arran Housing Study: Opportunities and Constraints: Report by Craigforth*, Irvine: North Ayrshire.

ONS (Office for National Statistics) (2008) *Scotland: Population Density by Local or Unity Authority* Newport: ONS, www.statistics.gov.uk/cci/nugget.asp?id=1082

Palmer, G, McInnes, T and Kenway, P (2006) *Monitoring Poverty and Social Exclusion in Scotland 2006*, York: Joseph Rowntree Foundation

Philip, K, Shucksmith, J and King, C (2004) *Sharing a Laugh? A Qualitative Study of Mentoring Interventions with Young People*, York: Joseph Rowntree Foundation, www.jrf.org.uk/publications/mentoring-vulnerable-young-people

Philo, C, Parr, H and Burns, N (2003) *Social Geographies of Rural Mental Health: Experiencing Inclusion and Exclusion* Glasgow: University of Glasgow, http://web.ges.gla.ac.uk/Projects/WebSite/Main.htm

Pierson, J (2008) *Going Local: Working in Communities and Neighbourhoods* London: Routledge.

Poole, D (2005) 'Rural Community-Building Strategies' in Lohmann, N and Lohmann, R (eds) *Rural Social Work Practice* New York, Columbia University Press.

Pugh, R (2000) *Rural Social Work* Lyme Regis: Russell House Publishing.

Pugh, R (2003), 'Considering the Countryside: Is There a Case for Rural Social Work?' *British Journal of Social Work*, **33(1)** pp. 67-85.

Pugh, R (2007) 'Dual Relationships: Personal and Professional Boundaries in Rural Social Work' *British Journal of Social Work*, **37(8)** pp.1405-23.

Pugh, R and Cheers, B (2010) *Rural Social Work: An International Perspective* Bristol: The Policy Press.

Pugh, R and Thompson N (1999) 'Social Work, Citizenship and Constitutional Change in the UK' *International Perspectives in Social Work: Social Work and the State* Brighton: Pavilion.

Pugh, R, Scharf, T, Williams, C and Roberts, D (2007) *Obstacles to Using and Providing Rural Social Care* London: Social Care Institute for Excellence.

Rollinson, P and Pardeck, J (2006) *Homelessness in Rural America: Policy and Practice* New York: The Haworth Press.

Save the Children/The Countryside Agency (2003) *Children and Domestic Violence in Rural Areas* London: Save the Children.

Schmidt, G. (2000) 'Remote Northern Communities: Implications for Social Work Practice' *International Social Work*, **43(3)** pp. 337-49.

Schmidt, G (2005) 'Geographic Context and Northern Child Welfare Practice' in Brownlee, K and Graham, J (eds) *Violence in the Family: Social Work Readings and Research from Northern and Rural Canada* Toronto: CSPI.

Scottish Consumer Council (2007) *Rural Advocacy in Scotland* Glasgow: Scottish Consumer Council.

Scottish Executive (2000) *Report of the Joint Future Working Group* Edinburgh: Scottish Executive, www.scotland.gov.uk/library3/social/rjfg-00.asp

Scottish Executive (2001) *Research Note RN01/114: Gypsy Travellers and Public Sector Policies* Edinburgh: Scottish Parliament Information Centre.

Scottish Executive (2002) *It's Everyone's Job to Make Sure I'm Alright*: *Report of the Child Protection and Audit Review* Edinburgh: The Stationery Office.

Scottish Executive (2003) *Social Focus on Urban Rural Scotland 2003* Edinburgh: Scottish Executive, www.scotland.gov.uk/Publications/2003/05/17207/22177

Scottish Executive (2005) *Getting it Right for Every Child: Proposals for Action* Edinburgh: Scottish Executive,

www.scotland.gov.uk/Publications/2005/06/20135608/56098

Scottish Executive (2006) *Changing Lives: Report of the 21st Century Social Work Review* Edinburgh: Scottish Executive.

Scottish Executive Social Research (2005) *Gypsy Travellers in Scotland: The Twice Yearly Count – No 7: January 2005* Edinburgh, Scottish Executive,

www.scotland.gov.uk/Resource/Doc/57346/0016455.pdf

Scottish Government (2008) *Self-directed Support (Direct Payments), Scotland, 2008* Edinburgh: Scottish Government,

www.scotland.gov.uk/Publications/2008/10/27092036/0

Scottish Government (2009a) *Scottish Government Urban Rural Classification* Edinburgh: Scottish Government,

www.scotland.gov.uk/Topics/Statistics/About/Methodology/UrbanRuralClassification

Scottish Government (2009b) *Scottish Government Urban Rural Classification 2007-2008* Edinburgh: Scottish Government,

www.scotland.gov.uk/Publications/2008/07/29152642/4

Scottish Government (2009c) *Rural Scotland Key Facts 2009* Edinburgh: Scottish Government,

www.scotland.gov.uk/Resource/Doc/285755/0087036.pdf

Scottish Government (2009d) 'More Rural Homes' News Release, 29 July,

www.scotland.gov.uk/News/Releases/2009/07/29105228

Scottish Government (2009e) *Consultation: National Eligibility Criteria for Adult Social Care and Waiting Times for Personal & Nursing Care* Edinburgh: Scottish Government,

www.scotland.gov.uk/Topics/Health/care/17655/research/NewPage

Scottish Government (2009f) *How Community Capacity Building Supports Community Empowerment* Edinburgh: Scottish Government,

www.scotland.gov.uk/Publications/2009/03/20155113/9

Scottish Government (2009g) *Rural Policy in Scotland: Rural Communities* Edinburgh: Scottish Government, www.scotland.gov.uk/Topics/farmingrural/Rural/rural-communities

Scottish Government (2009h) *Personalisation – A Shared Understanding; Commissioning for Personalisation; A Personalised Commissioning Approach to Support and Care Services* www.scotland.gov.uk/Publications/2009/04/07112629/0

Scottish Government (2009i) *Staff of Scottish Local Authority Social Work Services 2008* Edinburgh: Scottish Government, www.scotland.gov.uk/Publications/2009/06/23092957/8

Scottish Government (2009j) *Changing Scotland's Relationship with Alcohol: A Framework for Action* Edinburgh: Scottish Government, www.scotland.gov.uk/Resource/Doc/262905/0078610.pdf

Scottish Government (2009k) £2.4m to tackle domestic abuse, Press Release, www.scotland.gov.uk/News/Releases/2009/10/29110911

Scottish Government (2010a) *Abstract of Scottish Agricultural Statistics 1982 to 2009* Edinburgh: Scottish Government, www.scotland.gov.uk/Publications/2010/03/16160036/22

Scottish Government (2010b) *Criminal Justice Social Work Statistics, 2008-09, Additional Tables* Edinburgh: Scottish Government, www.scotland.gov.uk/Topics/Statistics/Browse/ Crime-Justice/Datasets/SocialWork

Scottish Government (2010c) *National Outcomes* Edinburgh: Scottish Government, www.scotland.gov.uk/About/scotPerforms/outcomes

Scottish Government Social Research (2009) *The Twice Yearly Count – No. 15: January 2009* Edinburgh: Scottish Government.

Scottish Island Network Newsletter (2003a), May, www.scottishislands.org.uk/Newsletters/2003_Newsletters

Scottish Island Network Newsletter (2003b) *Controversial Recommendation in Asylum Seekers Report*, September, www.scottishislands.org.uk/Downloads/newsletters/scottish-islands-network-newsletter-september-2003.doc

Scottish Office Central Research Unit (1998) *Social Work Research Findings No.15: Social Work and Criminal Justice: The National and Local Context* www.scotland.gov.uk/Publications/1998/12/e8d141df-4311-423b-b61b-99e9d589ef08

Scottish Parliament (2005a) *Equal Opportunities Official Report 21 June 2005* Edinburgh, Scottish Parliament, www.scottish.parliament.uk/business/committees/equal/or-05/eo05-1002.htm

Scottish Parliament (2005b) *Equal Opportunities Committee Report: Preliminary Findings on Gypsy Travellers – Review of Progress* Edinburgh, Scottish Parliament, www.scottish.parliament.uk/business/committees/equal/reports-05/eor05-05.htm

Scottish Social Services Council (2009), *Code of Practice for Social Service Workers* Dundee: Scottish Social Services Council, www.sssc.uk.com

Scoursfield, J (2003) *Gender and Child Protection,* Basingstoke: Palgrave.

Shelter (2004) *Priced Out – The Rising Cost of Rural Homes,* http://england.shelter.org.uk/__data/assets/pdf_file/0006/44835/Research_Report_Priced_Out_the_Rising_Cost_of_Rural_Homes_Oct_2004.pdf

Shu.cksmith, M. (2003) *Social Exclusion in Rural Areas: a review of Recent Research* Aberdeen: Arkleton Centre for Social Research, University of Aberdeen.

Smale, G and Bennett, W (1989) *Community Social Work in Scotland* London: National Institute for Social Work.

Smale, G, Tuson, G and Statham, D (2000) *Social Work and Social Problems: Working Towards Social Inclusion and Social Change* Basingstoke: MacMillan.

Smith, D (2002) 'Social Work with Offenders' in Adams, R, Dominelli, L and Payne, R (eds) *Social Work: Themes, Issues and Critical Debates* (2nd edition), Basingstoke: Macmillan.

Smith, J (2002) *Jessie's Journey* Edinburgh: Mercat.

Smith, J (2003) *Tales from the Tent* Edinburgh: Mercat.

Smith, J (2005) *Tears for a Tinker* Edinburgh: Mercat.

Smith, M and Homer, T (2009) *A Review of Service Development and Innovation in the Delivery of Joint Health and Social Care and Support Services in Rural and Remote Areas* Edinburgh: Health Scotland Joint Improvement Team, Remote and Rural Implementation Group, www.jitscotland.org.uk/action-areas/rural-and-remote/publications/

Smyth, M (1999) *New Ideas in Rural Development No 8: Tackling Crime in Rural Scotland* Edinburgh: The Stationery Office.

Southern Regional Educational Board Manpower Education and Training Project Rural Task Force (USA) (1998) 'Educational Assumptions for Rural Social Work' in Ginsberg, L (ed) *Social Work in Rural Communities* (3rd edition), Alexandria, VA: CSWE.

Stevenson, O (2005) 'Genericism and Specialisation: The story since 1970' *British Journal of Social Work* **35(5)** pp. 569-86.

SWIA (Social Work Inspection Agency) (2005) *An Inspection into the Care and Protection of Children in Eilean Siar* Edinburgh: Scottish Executive.

SWIA (Social Work Inspection Agency) (2006) *Performance Inspection: Comhairle nan Eilean Siar* Edinburgh: Scottish Executive.

SWIA (Social Work Inspection Agency) (2008) *Comhairle nan Eilean Siar Performance Inspection Follow-up Report October 2008* Edinburgh: Scottish Government.

SWIA (Social Work Inspection Agency) (2010) *Improving Social Work in Scotland* Edinburgh: Scottish Government, www.swia.gov.uk/swia/files/Overview_Report.pdf

Taggart, I (2008) 'One Scotland, Many Cultures?' *Thejournalonline – monthly magazine of the Law Society of Scotland*, www.journalonline.co.uk/Extras/1005097.aspx

Taylor, B (2004) 'Travellers in Britain: A Minority and the State', Historical Research **77(198)** pp. 575-96.

The Countryside Agency (2002) *Rural Proofing: Policy Makers Checklist*

Cheltenham: The Countryside Agency.

The Countryside Agency (2003) *Delivering Services to Children and Families in Rural Areas: The Early Lessons from Surestart* Wetherby: The Countryside Agency.

The Herald Newspaper (2008) 'Scottish gipsies [sic] not a separate ethnic group, tribunal rules', 13 March.

The Herald Newspaper (2009) 'House buyers pay more to live in the countryside', 12 September.

The Sun (2005) 'Stamp on the camps', 9 March, www.thesun.co.uk/sol/homepage/news/article104007.ece

The Sunday Times (2006) 'Stornoway's not racist, say Asians', October 8, www.timesonline.co.uk/tol/news/uk/scotland/article663308.ece

Thompson, N (2001) *Anti-Discriminatory Practice* (3rd edition) Basingstoke: Palgrave.

Tranter D (2005) 'Breaking the Connection Between Traditional Masculinity and Violence' in Brownlee, K and Graham, J *Violence in the Family: Social Work Readings and Research from Northern and Rural Canada,* Toronto: CSPI.

Turbett, C (2002) 'Calling the Shots: Innovations in Joint Working at a Local Level' Unpublished MSc Dissertation, University of Paisley.

Turbett, C (2004) 'A decade after Orkney: Towards a practice model for social work in the remoter areas of Scotland' *British Journal of Social Work* **34(7)** pp. 981-95.

Turbett, C (2006) 'Rural social work in Scotland and Eastern Canada: A comparison between the experiences of practitioners in remote communities' *International Journal of Social Work*, **49(5)** pp. 583-94.

Turbett C (2009a) 'Tensions in the delivery of social work services in rural and remote Scotland' *British Journal of Social Work*, **39(3)**, pp 506-21.

Turbett, C (2009b) 'Hard Travellin: The Fight for Scottish Gypsy Traveller Rights.' BASW *Rostrum* magazine, **87**.

Twigger, R (1998) *The Barnett Formula: Research Paper 98/8* London, House of Commons Library.

UNISON (2009) *Cash or Care? 10 Essential Questions for Councils on Personalisation* London: UNISON, www.unison.org.uk/acrobat/18493.pdf

UNISON Scotland and BASW (British Association of Social Workers) (2010) *Supervision and Workload Management for Social Work: A Negotiating Resource* Glasgow: UNISON.

Valentich, M (1996) 'Feminist Theory and Social Work Practice' in Turner, F (ed) *Social Work Treatment: Interlocking Theoretical Approaches* (4th Edition), New York: Free Press.

Van Cleemput, P and Parry, G (2001) 'Health Status of Gypsy Travellers' *Journal of Public Health Medicine*, **23(2)** pp. 129-34.

Wasko, N (2005) 'Wired for the Future? The Impact of Information and Telecommunications Technology on Rural Social Work' in Lohmann, N and Lohmann, R (eds) (2005) *Rural Social Work Practice* New York, Columbia University Press.

Waterhouse, L and McGhee, J (2002) 'Social Work in Scotland After Devolution' in Payne, M and Shardlow, S (eds) *Social Work in the British Isles* London: Jessica Kingsley Publishers.

Watkins, T (2004) 'Natural helping Networks – Assets for Rural Communities' in Laine Scales, T and Streeter, C (eds) *Rural Social Work: Building and Sustaining Community Assets* Belmont, CA: Thomson Brooks Cole.

Weiner, M and Petrella, P (2007) 'The Impact of New Technology: Implications for Social Work and Care Managers' in Aldgate, J, Healy, L, Malcolm, B, Pine, B, Rose, W and Seden, J (eds) *Enhancing Social Work Management: Theory and Best Practice from the UK and USA* London: Jessica Kingsley Publishers.

Wendt, S (2010) 'Building and Sustaining Local Co-ordination: An Australian Rural Community Responds to Domestic and Family Violence' *British Journal of Social Work* **40(1)** pp. 44-62.

Wendt, S and Cheers, B (2002) 'Impacts of Culture on Domestic Violence' *Rural Social Work* **7(1)** pp. 22-32.

White, S (2008) 'Drop the Deadline – Computers Can Hinder Child Protection' *The Guardian*, 19 November.

Wright, C (2000) 'Northern Spirit' *Community Practitioner* **73(4)** pp. 543-44.

York, R, Denton, R and Moran, J (1998) 'Rural and Urban Social Work Practice: Is there a difference?' in Ginsberg, L (ed) *Social Work in Rural Communities* (3rd edition), Alexandria, VA: CSWE.

Index